Watching Closely

WATCHING CLOSELY

A Guide to Ethnographic Observation

CHRISTENA NIPPERT-ENG

OXFORD
UNIVERSITY PRESS

OXFORD

UNIVERSITY PRESS

Oxford University Press is a department of the
University of Oxford. It furthers the University's objective
of excellence in research, scholarship, and education
by publishing worldwide.

Oxford   New York
Auckland   Cape Town   Dar es Salaam   Hong Kong   Karachi
Kuala Lumpur   Madrid   Melbourne   Mexico City   Nairobi
New Delhi   Shanghai   Taipei   Toronto

With offices in
Argentina   Austria   Brazil   Chile   Czech Republic   France   Greece
Guatemala   Hungary   Italy   Japan   Poland   Portugal   Singapore
South Korea   Switzerland   Thailand   Turkey   Ukraine   Vietnam

Oxford is a registered trade mark of Oxford University Press
in the UK and in certain other countries.

Published in the United States of America by
Oxford University Press
198 Madison Avenue, New York, NY 10016

© Oxford University Press 2015

Library of Congress Cataloging-in-Publication Data
Nippert-Eng, Christena E.
 Watching closely : a guide to ethnographic observation / Christena Nippert-Eng.
     pages cm
 Includes bibliographical references and index.
 ISBN 978-0-19-023551-2 (hbk. : alk. paper)—ISBN 978-0-19-023552-9 (pbk. : alk. paper)
 1. Observation (Psychology)   I. Title.
 BF323.O2N57 2015
 305.80072'3–dc23
                                    2015006800

9 8 7 6 5 4 3 2 1
Typeset in Dante MT Std
Printed in the United States of America
on acid-free paper

For Peter, the One and Only

CONTENTS

This book is an exercise-based, practical guide designed to help fieldworkers get better at observation-based research. I wrote it primarily for students in the social and behavioral sciences who study human and (other) animal populations, as well as for user-centered designers, architects, and urban planners. You should find this book useful if you would like to do any of the following:

1. strengthen your core skills and mindset as a fieldworker;
2. focus more attention on the visual part of the field;
3. experiment with more creative ways of collecting, analyzing, and communicating your data;
4. base your fieldwork even more consciously on your favorite concepts, collecting data that more directly reflects your interests and challenges your assumptions;
5. work in a more focused and efficient, "mission-directed" way while in the field;
6. bring a more analytical approach to the entirety of your fieldwork process;
7. produce more scientifically rigorous and persuasive research;
8. develop concrete, high-level expectations about what ethnographic data are and how it might be used;
9. apply observational methods to a larger, more diverse, shorter-term collection of problems and settings; and
10. reflect on your personal research process in a detailed, systematic way.

Ethnographers rely on three related activities to conduct research in the field: observation, conversation, and participation. Directly observing others in their environments then using the resulting data to develop and share our insights is an essential part of our toolkit. We draw on observation skills regardless of the substantive focus of our research or whether we aspire to more positivist/realist or more critical, interpretive, or impressionist outcomes (Van Maanen 2010, Vaughan 2009).

Yet too few of us have been taught how to acquire useful, rigorous observational data and then re-present that data for effective analysis and communication. As a result, ethnographers' observational muscles tend to be our weakest. If we pay even a little extra attention to strengthening these muscles, I believe we will achieve a significant payoff in the quality of our work.

Observation can offer solid evidence of demonstrated behaviors occurring within a specific environment at a specific time. Observational skills help, for instance, when we want to (1) use people's actions to independently verify their spoken claims; (2) describe and make sense of what is happening when no one can—or will—talk with us; and (3) better capture higher-level patterns of behavior especially regarding objects and environments. Systematic, observation-based data can help us both find out what is actually going on and justify our claims to others. But observation only gives clues and partial answers as to *why* things happen and the meanings actors attribute to them. This is why direct observation should be combined with other methods of understanding to address most ethnographers' problems of interest.[1]

My goal is to make this possible. I want to help readers get as good at direct observation as they are at the other methods on which most graduate programs focus. Accordingly, the core of *Watching Closely* is a series of exercises and reflections designed to improve your understanding of the observational craft and enlarge your skill-set in acquiring, analyzing, and conveying observational data.

When I was working on my PhD in sociology, graduate students generally received little training in how to do fieldwork. Mostly, we read books based on ethnographic research and then we talked about the books. We sat around tables, discussing the authors' appendices, various interviewing techniques, problems of access, ethics, and relationship building, and the risks of "going native." At the end of the term, we dispersed to our individual field sites and began our research.

These discussions were interesting and valuable. But they were not enough. As soon as I landed my first job, I decided to design for my own students the kinds of methods courses I wished had been available to me. It has been an exciting challenge to take what I have learned since then and turn it into a book, so I can share my approach more broadly. What you find here may be quite different from anything you've seen before, but I hope it will prove useful in your own journey as a fieldworker.

ACKNOWLEDGMENTS

I want to extend my profound thanks to:

My hearty, courageous, and clever students, especially those who have so graciously allowed me to share their exceptional work through the sample responses found on the Oxford University Press website as well as throughout this book: Saad Alghamdi, Jorge Angarita, Kristine Angell, Lauren Braun, Betina De Gorordo, Caroline DeWick, Alia Fadel, Daniya Kamran, Karolina Kohler, David LaPorte, Sarah Norell, Matt Otten, Chiho Sasaki, Jennifer Sculley, John Shin, Stephanie Smith, Jeff Turkelson, Helen Wills, Janice Wong, and especially John Dominski, Fred Grier, Jim Hornor, and Eugene and Sally Limb, who also became my beloved coauthors on *Gorillas Up Close* (2016).

The dedicated keepers and researchers at the Regenstein Center for African Apes, especially Andy Henderson (sadly, recently passed away) and Kristen Lukas, who made my first class in 1998 feel so welcome; Dominic Calderisi, Jill Moyse, and Maureen Leahy, who do so now; and the public relations staff at Lincoln Park Zoo.

The objects of our mutual affection, respect, and study: the gorillas of Lincoln Park Zoo, who are not only (usually) gracious in allowing us to learn from them, but who occasionally attend class, joining our discussion circle from the other side of the glass. I feel a deep connection with some of these individuals and an abiding fascination with all of them.

Five anonymous reviewers, Sally Augustin, Simon Brauer, Mary Chayko, Gary Fine, Terry Izzo, Simona Maschi, Noah McClain, Harvey Molotch, Judy Wittner, and Eviatar Zerubavel, for their helpful feedback on an early draft of the book and enthusiastic support.

The members of Gary Fine's Ethnography Workshop at Northwestern University, who also gave me important, early feedback, especially Gemma Mangione and Lisa-Jo Van den Scott.

John Dominski, Gitte Jonsdatter, Chiho Sasaki, and Jennifer Sculley, for permission to share their always-inspiring work in this book.

Fen Truitt, a remarkable young artist, for her wonderful illustrations and the delight of working with her.

My dear friend Mary Ruth Yoe, whose generosity and brilliant editorial prowess are simply unsurpassed.

James Cook, who is surely every author's idea of the perfect, treasured editor. He has been an avid supporter of this project from the moment we first discussed it. I have benefitted enormously from his time, attention, care, and patience, as well as his excellent capacity for solving problems in ways both creative and pragmatic.

My entire family, but especially my parents, Tena and Vic Nippert, who first fanned the flames of my interest in watching nonhumans closely; Gretchen Eng (and friends) for hours of much-needed comic relief while I worked on this; Catherine Eng, for her thoughtful interest in this work over many years and, more recently, for the delightful design concept, initial layouts, and art direction of this book; and Peter Eng, who did all the things wonderful husbands do for their wives while I was working on this but who also invented a portable tabletop standing desk for me and then headed to the drop zone—exactly when I needed him to do both.

Note

1. Michele Lamont and Ann Swidler's view of being "against methodological tribalism," and in favor of letting the problem in which one is interested drive the approaches one selects to study the problem is the only sensible approach (2014, 154–55).

ABOUT THE COMPANION WEB SITE

http://global.oup.com/us/watchingclosely

Oxford has created a Website to accompany *Watching Closely*. Here you will find sample responses by Dr. Nippert-Eng's former students to the exercises contained in this book along with brief introductions that highlight specific features of each response. Readers are encouraged to consult this resource only after trying each of the exercises, themselves, in order to allow for as much personal creativity and innovation as possible.

Watching Closely

Part One:
Getting Ready

How to Use This Book

How to Do the Exercises

This book is based on the model of a fine arts or studio course. Such courses focus on essential skills and are organized around well-defined challenges or exercises, to which students respond in whatever way seems appropriate to them. Each exercise in this book focuses on a particular concept and a specific data-collecting challenge. Readers are invited to respond as creatively as possible in whatever way seems to best address the given problem. With each exercise, the level of challenge increases, with subsequent exercises inviting you to build on what you have learned. The discussions around each exercise get shorter, too, as successive exercises assume what was covered earlier.

Readers will get the most out of these exercises by actually doing them, one at a time. Each exercise begins with a discussion of the central concept and data-taking goals, followed by the observation assignment. When you reach this point, stop reading and do the exercise. Spend a solid sixty minutes in the field, no more. Later—sometimes, the next day—write up what you learned during your time in the field. I'll provide a suggested structure for this write-up, to help focus your attention on some of each exercise's most important aspects.

Take the report writing seriously. Imagine you are a student taking this class with me and must turn in your response for feedback. Once you have your report in hand, return to the book and pick up where you left off. Armed with the insights gained during your time in the field, the data you collected, and your report summarizing your experience, use the follow-up discussion about the exercise to make further sense of your work.

Each post-exercise discussion highlights some of the especially important conceptual, mechanical, and representational aspects of the exercise. I review the problems you most likely encountered and some choices you might have made in your response to these problems. I also provide tips for what to keep in mind as you move forward.

Following the post-exercise discussion, you may wish to visit this book's companion website at http://global.oup.com/watchingclosely. There, you will see additional responses to the exercise produced by former students. A short introduction to each sample response directs your attention to features that you may find of special interest.

I strongly recommend that you do not look at the sample responses before you do the exercise and write the report, yourself. Self-discovery is what this journey is all about. Tackling the work unencumbered by someone else's choices makes your own innovations more likely. It also helps things stick in a way that replicating someone else's solution does not.

When you have completed these exercises, you will have a collection of data-filled reports memorializing your experiences in and about the field. Each exercise can be done independently, whenever you have time. Done in the same field site and taken all together, your reports also can be seen as chapters, each building on the next as a string of related investigations. You can revisit any of these exercises again and again, getting something new out of it each time you do it, whatever your observation site.

You can also design exercises for yourself, tailored to future projects. This book is not intended to be a comprehensive collection of exercises, readings, or reflections. Rather, it is an introduction to a way of thinking about fieldwork meant to help you produce your own, even more inventive applications.

The approach I offer is specifically designed so that the quest for scientific rigor, the core of a researcher's chosen discipline, and an individual's unique talents and experience can each enhance the other. No two people have quite the same ways of seeing or of making sense of what they see. No two people have precisely the same interests. No two people have the same skills for envisioning, capturing, and re-presenting data. This is why even if they're looking at exactly the same scene in exactly the same field no two people will produce the same results for any of these exercises. Their work should be entirely consistent with and useful to each other. However, their end results could be even radically different—a fact that should be celebrated.

Selecting Your Field and Study Population

(Nonhuman) Animals Are Best

I have been developing the method on which this book is based for some time now, in a course I teach to design, architecture, engineering, and natural and social science students. The classes take place at Lincoln Park Zoo in Chicago, where we study the gorillas.

The course is not offered by Lincoln Park Zoo. The scientists and animal care specialists there kindly welcome us as they do any member of the public. But the work we do is entirely independent of theirs. In short, nothing you read here in any way reflects the expertise or involvement of the remarkable professionals at Lincoln Park Zoo.

If you go online and look at former students' responses to these exercises, you will see them struggling to tell the gorillas apart, much less accurately describe and understand what they are doing. A lot of the information and assertions—especially in the earlier exercises—is just wrong. The students are working off only what they observe—no secondary research allowed. They're in the process of learning how to see better and take better data, too. They are not supposed to be fluent regarding gorilla behavior, the observation process, or best practices in zoo research design.

So why do I teach the course at the zoo? There are several reasons that nonhuman animals—especially ones with which the researcher is not overly familiar—are preferable subjects. First, by now, you've learned *not* to notice an awful lot of things about people. It would be rude to really pay attention to much of what any given person presents to us at any given time. Moreover, among the things we do notice about other people, very little actually makes a notable impression on us. Something may register somewhere below the conscious level and from there, it may well influence our thoughts. However, as cognitive scientist (and popular animal behaviorist) Alexandra Horowitz (2014) so vividly demonstrates, much of what we can perceive rarely becomes the focus of conscious reflection.[1]

When it comes to watching people, even the small subset of things that we both notice and to which we consciously pay attention may not be very useful for improving observation skills. The problem is that we may assume we know what's going on with those things and substitute what we *think* people are doing for what they're *actually* doing. We may try to substitute our assumptions of *why* they're doing it for what they're actually doing. When we think we know the reason why someone is doing something, we often cognitively override or ignore the actual behaviors in which they're engaged.[2]

Worse, if we don't have prior explanations of what people are doing or if we can't immediately discern the reason they're doing something, then we may try to get them to tell us. In our desire to understand what's happening, the temptation may be to cheat, substituting conversation for observation, rather than forcing ourselves to watch and listen harder or in a different way. Lacking the anthropological option of watching humans living in ways that are truly strange and speaking languages completely unknown to us, our best bet for practicing observation skills is to observe nonhuman animals.

Chances are, there is a species living nearby to which you haven't dedicated years of close study. It should be an animal or group of animals about which you do not assume you know everything. It can be a nest of birds or squirrels, a tank of fish in your living room or a local pet store, a regular group of canine friends at the park, some horses, cows, or goats in a field, or an exotic species at the local zoo—whatever is available and interesting to you.

One unexpected payoff to watching nonhumans is that once we spend time closely studying other animals, it's easier to think of ourselves as a different species. We start taking less about ourselves for granted, able to better see what we actually do. Behavioral and possibly motivational similarities between other species and our own become apparent. This helps us to challenge our usual explanations about why our human subjects do what they do—as well as our tendency to privilege our own species over others.

Observing People Also Works

That said, you *can* do these exercises with people as your focus of attention. Studying people is probably the end goal for most—but not all—of this book's readers. If you decide to focus on people for these exercises, you'll want to find a place where people don't mind being watched and don't mind you being the one to do it. In fact, sociologist David Grazian (2012) found the zoo an excellent place to unobtrusively observe *people*. Wherever you go, you'll need to feel free to take notes and to be seen doing so, consistent with your Institutional Review Board's (IRB) expectations, if applicable.

Captive, indigenous, and domesticated animals may be found in places designed for us to watch them. If you're respectful, they won't mind you doing so, and you can usually be quite comfortable in the process. It's another reason for studying nonhumans—especially since you don't need IRB approval to do so. With people, it can be a little harder to find the right place—and time—to do this.

One summer, for instance, I found a way to productively pass time in airports while waiting for flights. I began watching traffic patterns and the waiting behaviors of other passengers, sketching and taking notes on what I saw. I was following the advice of my drawing instructor, who recommended practicing as often as possible, whenever one had a few minutes to spare. I became fascinated by the activities I saw: ground crews servicing planes and managing luggage and mail, pilots doing visual checks, attendants coming and going between gate doors and service counters. The flurry of focused activity inside and outside the terminals was an engaging challenge for my improving observation and sketching skills.

Unfortunately, this was the summer of 2001. I had hardly begun my airport observational habit when the transformative events of 9/11 occurred. My more obvious studies of airport logistics instantly came to a halt. There are places and times when overt observation activity may get you into big trouble.

Thus, if you're going to focus on people for these exercises, it's best to find something like a busy coffee shop, library, mall, or park. Choose a place where people expect to see anonymous others writing, reading, watching, and sketching. This will make it less likely that anyone will notice you, mistake your intentions, or feel threatened by what you are doing.

I recommend that you carry a business card and do not try to hide your activity. It is difficult if not impossible to do these exercises without being openly engaged in the process. You may not want to draw attention to what you're doing, but primates seem to have a sixth sense for someone trying to keep a secret. Chances are, if you're open about your activity, people will assume you are a researcher of some kind and completely legitimate in whatever you're doing—and they'll be right. You may have to be willing to show them what you're doing, though, to assuage their concerns— and respect their curiosity.

Figure 1.1. Makari inspecting my notes. Photo by John Dominski

Whichever You Pick, Go for Flow

Whatever species you observe for these exercises, there is one more thing to consider as you decide who or what to focus on. Because the exercises are designed to help you strengthen your existing fieldwork skills, you'll need to focus on a species, a set of behaviors, and an environment that do not leave you feeling over- or underwhelmed by the challenge they pose. You also should find your choice inherently interesting.

I'll use social psychologist Mihaly Csikszentmihalyi's work on "flow" to explain why. In his seminal book on the subject, *Beyond Boredom and Anxiety*, Csikszentmihalyi (1975) studied rock climbers in order to explore our perception of time. Interested in our ability to become so engrossed in an activity that we lose the perception of time passing, he argued that this is at least partly the result of the match between the level of challenge one faces and the level of skill one possesses. If the challenge associated with an activity is too low, he argues, we are likely to feel bored. We have a heightened sense of time, because it drags—our skill level is too high to feel fully engaged by the too-simple challenge at hand. If the challenge is too high—because our skill level is too low—then we are also likely to have a heightened sense of time. In this case, we feel anxious. Time goes by much too quickly as we worry about the fact that we must perform but are not up to the challenge at hand.

Csikszentmihalyi argues that it is when the challenge meets our current skill level—or, better, slightly exceeds it—that we become fully engaged. The wonderful experience of "flow" sets in and we lose all perception of time. Perhaps hours after starting a task, we suddenly look up and realize just how much time has passed while we were gloriously lost in what we were doing, oblivious to everything else.

Strive for flow while doing these exercises. Creating the structural opportunity for it is not easy. Start by turning off your cell phone and going to a place where no one knows you. Find an observation subject that is a good match for you too, inducing neither boredom nor anxiety. It should be a good fit with your current skill level as an observer and recorder of what you see. It's even better if you can watch individuals who cannot speak to you, bump into you, or make any demands on you as you watch them.

Flow is not only a function of the match between challenge and skill. Your choice of field also should be interesting to you. Csikszentmihalyi studied people who, by definition, found rock climbing interesting. If you don't, then what are your chances of finding flow while rock climbing, even if you match the challenge to your skill level?

On this point, when Csikszentmihalyi and social scientist Rick Robinson (1990) took their interest in understanding experiences to art museums, they found that the ability to appreciate what one is seeing can be a significant barrier to an individual's ability to actually see it. Visitors need an entry point, some way to appreciate some aspect of a painting, for instance, or they will not try to engage it further. Similarly, until students can consistently identify a single gorilla or a specific behavior, they have a very hard time actually seeing, just *seeing*, what is going on in front of them. Recognizing the *meaning* of what one is seeing only comes after much more study. This is a common problem for entering practically any research location. It is why the sequence of exercises in this book demonstrates how to find a failsafe entry point into any field—a way to begin seeing what's going on—then systematically develop your expertise about it.

Balancing our interests and our ability is a fundamental tension for fieldworkers who want to get better at our craft. The more my subject interests me, the more likely I am to pay close attention to it. Yet sometimes what is fascinating to me is beyond my skills as a fieldworker. Animals like the white-cheeked gibbons at Lincoln Park Zoo, for instance—smart, gregarious, physically powerful—are very high energy. I could watch them all day. But I wish anyone good luck in closely capturing what they do. There are slow, extremely calm subjects, whose activity is much easier to document. For me, these include dromedaries and zebras that twitch at flies for what seem like hours—or any nocturnal animal during the day. Technically it's an easier job for me to record and re-present their activity. But at this point, none of these animals sustains my interest for an entire hour. Trying to do these exercises in either situation—fascinating (to me) but hard to capture, or boring (to me) but easy to capture—would mean fighting against myself.

Fortunately, other animals fit the bill perfectly for me: western lowland gorillas. Not only are they utterly fascinating (to me), but they also live their lives at a pace that I find manageable as I try to document them. Every once in a while they throw in a flurry of activity that I find terrifically challenging, leaving me either satisfyingly energized or wonderfully frustrated. My time spent watching them reminds me that I still have much to learn about them, the observational craft, and how to gather useful data in useful ways—as well as how much I enjoy doing exactly that.

Gorillas seem to be an excellent match for other people, too, and so I ask my students to study the gorillas who live at Lincoln Park Zoo while they do these exercises. The zoo is free, open 365 days a year, and easily accessible via mass transit. One can sit shoulder to shoulder with the gorillas, separated only by glass, in a beautiful, spacious, climate-controlled building. As soon as the weather gets cold, there are very few other visitors and so we also get to more or less call the space our own.

Try different observational venues to find one that is inviting, interesting, and right for you. This book is meant to help you understand your own process, preferences, and aversions as a field-worker. It's meant to help you understand what you are already drawn to and what you might like to add to your repertoire of questions, tools, and techniques. Selecting an engaging but challenge-appropriate subject to watch in a place that's comfortable for you will be an important part of this self-discovery process.

There's also nothing like discovering something about yourself alongside someone else doing the same activity. Training partners are not just for athletes. You might want to get a friend or two to do these exercises with you. It can be quite enjoyable when everyone has their own mission but shares a common focus to their work. I love teaching about observation when I am right there in the field with my students and we can all see and talk about the same things. A regular trip to a farm, aquarium, zoo, or city park with a friend is great for fostering camaraderie and breaking up an otherwise unremarkable semester as well as upping your ethnographic game.

How hard will this be? Will it be worth it?

This may be a very different approach to fieldwork than that to which you are accustomed. The start-up costs may seem high. Most of my students think the payoff is well worth the investment. But it is not for the faint of heart. You must be willing to step out of your comfort zone if you want to tackle these exercises. You will need a good sense of humor about yourself, a fair amount of patience, and the desire to tap into your most adventurous and scientific sides to take full advantage of what you'll find here. But if you can give it just a few weeks of your life, you might find this approach transformative.

Depending on your background and learning style, the time you spend could feel challenging, liberating, or both. Fieldworkers who study (nonhuman) animal behavior, space- or object-use, computer-human interaction, and systems of production may have an easier time with some parts of these exercises than more classically trained social and behavioral scientists. The latter typically bring a distinctive set of theories and concepts to the field, though, and this can provide its own advantage—as can the abilities of those who are comfortable with drawing, photography, and the design of diagrams.

No matter what your background, the nine exercises focus on concepts and skillsets that should be useful for most ethnographers. We will start by watching what happens in the field across time and across space. Two exercises are dedicated to each of these concepts. For the remaining exercises, we turn to the kinds of matters to which cultural ethnographers and those who focus on small group interactions tend to be drawn: objects, relationships, power, and play.

In general, you will find here a more structured framework for your research. It can help give you a fast and useful overview of a specific population or location, getting you started when all the possibilities might feel most overwhelming. It can help you focus precisely on an activity or object that has captured your imagination, or to break up your regular routine in the field if your research starts to feel a bit stale. It can also help you think at a higher level about your subjects and the activities, objects, and environments in which you are interested. It can help you wrap up at the end of your research, too, making sure you've gotten the most out of your time in the field. This framework can, in other words, help you target the data and creative space where meaningful innovation is most possible—in theory, methods, and knowledge or in services, products, and policies—and at any point in your research process.

Notes

1. In this stunning collection of essays, Horowitz shows that just by walking around her neighborhood with different experts, she begins to see all kinds of things that have, in fact, always been there.
2. For an interesting read on the general phenomena of what we intentionally do not pay attention to, see Zerubavel 2006.

A Different Approach to Fieldwork

In this section, I describe the scientific, creative, and ambitious approach to field research that lies at the heart of this book. I also discuss what it means to be a well-prepared fieldworker. While the section serves as a comprehensive introduction to these issues, I elaborate on these matters within the context of each exercise as well.

A Scientific, Creative, and Ambitious Approach

Throughout this book, I advocate for an approach to fieldwork that is

- *scientific*, where fieldwork reflects a commitment to systematic observation, a well-defined analytical perspective, the use of a daily, mission-driven approach to gathering data, and the clear and clever operationalization of key concepts to produce work that is more rigorous, amenable to peer review, and transcends any specific project;
- *creative*, drawing on observation-based work and our capacity to envision, acquire, and convey data in original, compelling ways to capitalize on individual researchers' unique talents and perspectives; and

- *ambitious*, extending ethnography's reach and increasing its efficiency and effectiveness while addressing a more diverse set of problems than those associated with more traditional forms of fieldwork.

Scientific Fieldwork

The classification, possibilities, and goals of ethnographic research as a scientific endeavor have been a source of sometimes heated debate. Sociologist John Van Maanen (2010) offers an accessible survey of the different views of ethnography that have emerged over the past few decades, arguing that this "most humanistic of the social sciences and most scientific of the humanities" continues to embrace remarkably diverse approaches.

The debate about whether or not ethnography is a scientific enterprise stems from two main sets of considerations. First, there are differences in interlocutors' understandings of fieldwork and ethnographic data, in part based on differing views about the relationship between what is seen and the individual who sees it. Second, there are differences among practitioners about the proper uses and goals of ethnography. Lurking underneath both concerns are divergent, often unarticulated views of "science."

My own philosophical stance toward fieldwork is best summarized as that of a moderate social constructivist (Berger and Luckmann 1968) or, even better, a dialectical critical realist (e.g., Bhaskar 1975; Gorski 2013). In short, I believe there is an objective reality out there. However, as many scholars of science and knowledge have argued—and many ethnographers have demonstrated—the ways we see the world and the senses we make of it are mediated by the ways we have been taught to do so. An individual researcher may pursue an unmediated truth but it is not possible to obtain it. This is because we perceive the world through an intersubjective lens shaped by our life experiences, including the cognitive frameworks with which we have been taught to think.

As scientists, we are aware that our perception of the world is mediated and that it can be difficult to separate what is real from our interpretations of it. We also understand that what we see and how we make sense of it is likely to differ between individuals. But this does not stop us from trying to apprehend reality and figure out how and why things work. Scientists commit to methodological and comparative techniques to constantly review, challenge, and build upon each other's claims. The unique perspectives of individual researchers—and the disparities between them—serve as assets that move our collective understanding forward. Through rigorous, self-conscious review we slowly and carefully amend our understanding of reality, and use our constantly evolving understandings to engage in future iterations of sense-making. In this way science challenges yet continues to build upon itself, primarily through very small steps, sometimes in larger ones (Kuhn 1970; Popper 2002).

At its most general level, "science" is defined by its commitment to systematic observation and the methods, theory, and knowledge that generate and stem from it. It does not matter if we study the atoms on a surface substrate, the distant nebula of space, or the behavior of cancer cells, bees, or people going about their daily business. If we are scientists, what matters is that we do so through systematic observation, using whatever wavelengths of light, techniques, concepts, and knowledge appropriate to our subject.

Ethnographers may not identify as scientists. I do. There are plenty who do not. In 2010 the ethnocentric and sometimes unethical work of past anthropologists as well as the very different nature of their colleagues' work in physical anthropology led some cultural anthropologists to make a compelling case for distancing themselves from the scientific tradition of their discipline. Previously, the goal of the American Anthropological Association's long-range plan was "to advance anthropology as the science that studies humankind in all its aspects." Today, the association's stated goal is "to advance public understanding of humankind in all its aspects" (Wade 2010). Plenty of ethnographers in sociology also consider themselves more akin to activists, humanists, and other interpretive storytellers than to scientists per se.

Whether or not an ethnographer self-identifies as a social scientist, these exercises will be useful. However, they were designed especially to help those who embrace the identity of social scientist (or, in the case of designers, architects, and others, user of social scientific methods) better approach the fundamental tenets of scientific rigor. Social scientists who are also fieldworkers have much in common with folklorists, documentarians, journalists, and humanists of many kinds. If we are also scientists, however, we must focus on and adhere to an additional set of standards and goals.

Like other scientists, ethnographers have a great deal of freedom to decide what we will investigate and how we will do it. We can define our interests however we choose. We can decide what are data. We can use and represent that data in whatever way we wish. Like all scientists, our peers will judge us on our choices.

Like other scientists, we also realize that we cannot access an objective reality except through our particular interpretive lens. Accordingly, we pursue our truth as carefully and systematically as we can, keeping the reality of our interpretive lenses in mind, and prepared to be properly constrained by the truths of others. Collectively, this is how we continue to zero in on the objective, concrete parts of reality. In the process, we repeatedly confirm sociologist John Martin's (2011, 341) observation that "the concrete, far from being the obvious and the given, is the focus of bitter controversy and sometimes only emerges after painful elaborative work on the part of the analyst." This is indeed a good description of what is at the heart of what we call science.

Where ethnographers may differ from other scientists, I would argue, is in a need to refresh our commitment to science. The richly descriptive, interpretive stories, as well as the objects, services, and other products we create could only be better for it. This means looking with a keen eye for opportunities to translate the commitment to science—to systematic observation and the knowledge, theory, and methods associated with it—into new ways of engaging in our craft. Given the limitations of social science, and especially of fieldwork, the ways we commit to scientific principles will look different from those of a chemist in a lab or an astronomer viewing the heavens. However, we can go a long way in stiffening our scientific spines by adopting practices that make our fieldwork more explicitly analytical, mission-driven, concept-based, and empirical.

Analytical

Careful analysis of one's data is key to the scientific enterprise. There is a well-established literature on the analytic nature of ethnographic work. Sociologist John Lofland's (1995, 30) description of "analytic ethnography," for instance, emphasizes ethnographers' systematic analysis of the foci of their research, addressing questions common to social scientists regardless of methodological approach:

1. *Type?* What is it? What are its defining features and its varieties?
2. *Frequency?* How often does it occur?
3. *Magnitude?* What is its size, strength, or intensity?

4. *Structure?* What is its detailed organization?
5. *Process?* How does it operate?
6. *Cause?* How does it come to be?
7. *Consequence?* What does it affect?
8. *Agency?* How do people strategize in or toward it?

For sociologist Diane Vaughan (2009, 688), "analytical ethnography" is but one strain of "analytical sociology," which, as a social scientific approach,

> urges a turning away from variable-centered approaches toward strategies that produce explanations of events and outcomes by revealing the mechanisms that generate the observed relationships. It is designed to examine key social processes and break them down into their primary components, showing how they work together to produce outcomes. The focus shifts from variables to actors, actions, and the "cogs and wheels" that respond to and reproduce social phenomena. Arriving at explanation is the goal.

As Vaughn shows, precisely what one is trying to explain can vary tremendously between ethnographers. What is constant is ethnographers' commitment to analytically, systematically break down and then explain whatever it is that they've observed.

Sociologist Jack Katz (2001, 84) has argued that throughout this process, ethnographers often pursue their questions and explanations through the research logic of "analytic induction." Ethnographers "collect data, develop analysis, and organize the presentation of research findings . . . [in order to produce] a specification of the individually necessary and jointly sufficient conditions for the emergence of some part of social life." Like other scientists, ethnographers analyze the specific in great detail, Katz argues, to develop and arrive at more general conclusions.

The analytical dimension of science does not apply only after one begins to collect data; it also applies in the preparatory work that helps a researcher first decide what to look at and how to do so. Thus, to this more mainstream understanding of the analytical nature of ethnography, we may add the possibilities offered by formal sociologist Eviatar Zerubavel (1980) with his view of "analytical fieldwork." Zerubavel (1980, 31) argues that ethnographers should conscientiously develop and capitalize on a specific "analytic framework" before entering the field:

> The act of establishing the particular analytical concerns and focus of the study must precede the act of entering the field, because it is the focus of one's concerns that determines, to a large extent, the boundaries of one's perception (Pike 1967, 98–119, quoted in Zerubavel 1980). Researchers' particular analytical concerns and foci provide their observations with the particular cognitive orientation that is necessary in order to decide what to regard as "relevant" for their purposes (and, therefore, notable), and what to ignore as "irrelevant." These concerns and foci must be established prior to the beginning of the study, since they essentially function as *sensitizers* which help researchers "see" patterns which might have never emerged in mere perception. In other words, researchers would have probably missed and ignored many patterns had they not been particularly concerned with particular analytical foci.

As a practicing ethnographer, the most important implication of this liberating view for me is that the strength of my data will depend as much on the clarity of my theoretical and conceptual interests *before* I enter the field as on my ability to query, capture, and re-present what I see once I'm there. To get the most systematic, comprehensive, and useful data possible to address one's interests, one *must* clarify what those interests are—first. Indeed, if one cannot pay attention to everything in the field, then why not decide beforehand what one is truly interested in and pay close attention to that? We should focus our lens as sharply as we can, then take it to the field and use it to view whatever is available through the best, most well-honed set of optics possible.

With this approach, fieldworkers can truly hit the ethnographic ground running. Other types of scientists usually do not begin their experiments until they know enough of what interests them that they can design an effective way to get the data that will let them explore it further. Similarly, fieldworkers should identify at least some initial concepts, system components, behaviors, or small, fact-based questions in which we are interested. Then, and only then, we should start to design our time in the field around these interests. Of course we will continue to hone our foci of attention, interpretive lenses, and research plans as our projects mature. But a strong, focused entry to the field can make all the difference in propelling a project forward, whatever shape it eventually takes.

Naturally, putting in the scholarly effort upfront means getting comfortable with delaying the start of our fieldwork. Delaying because one is honing one's interests is different from delaying because of fear or procrastination. The payoff from more careful conceptual planning can be substantial. We can avoid wasting time in the field and adding to any anxiety we might have about our progress, increasing our chances of finishing the project and in less time, overall. The result can be correct, compelling, and sometimes extremely bold and original research, in part because one commits so thoroughly to thinking deeply about what one is truly interested in, right from the start.

As an analytical fieldworker, for me the whole point of watching closely is to think closely. I observe to help drill down into the deepest detail of what is available to me. Watching the field helps me mentally explore what I am interested in. What I see is an entry point into the systems of which it is a part—the social (including cognitive), physical, natural, and artificial structures in which it is embedded. Watching closely in the field thus allows me to focus my attention in an organic, often unexpected way on fundamental principles, processes, relationships, and organizing features that I might not encounter otherwise.

I especially like the self-discovery aspect of this approach. I like watching an interaction, an object, or a space and trying to wrap my mind around it. I use my analytical focus of attention to generate as many hypotheses and challenges as possible to what I think might be going on. The things in my head are more exciting when I see something unexpected in the outside world, too, and, then realize (à la sociologist Howie Becker) "Aha! That's an example of *that!*" and then, "OK, so what does that mean about this other thing, too?"

The enlightening capacity of the field only works if one commits to savoring one's time there and the potential revelations that await therein. To fully exploit these possibilities each data point must be viewed as a portal into as many others as we can. The more we linger over something we see or hear, the more we try to trace its connection to other things we've smelled, touched, seen, heard, or tasted—the more we can think closely about any one thing we encounter in the field—the richer and more innovative our work is likely to be. This ability to see the details of life around us and to imagine how they are connected is what fieldworkers share with the finest writers, artists, inventors, therapists, doctors, car mechanics, intelligence analysts, animal whisperers, and all other types of acute observers and clever problem solvers.

The capacity to see details and imagine how they are connected can make ethnography an excellent methodological approach for case studies, given one's definition of a case (Ragin 1992). Case studies are especially useful for understanding process—showing us the how—and often the why—behind the what. If we want to understand how *pervasive* the how and the what are, we must turn to other methods and approaches. Ethnographers cannot claim the generalizable, reproducible, highly predictive, population-wide results of some of our colleagues' techniques. But we are able to provide remarkably deep understanding of our field sites, the processes embedded in them, and how individual elements combine to create a particular whole.

By the time you finish this book, you will realize how much my commitment to watching closely is driven by the desire to think closely. Close thinking should be the core of any ethnographic study. At its best, fieldworkers use their theoretically informed, analytical perspective as a filter at all times, informing and informed by any and every moment of the observation process. Sometimes, we think closely about and comprehend the meaning of what we're seeing right at the point of capture. These epiphanies are especially sweet. Sometimes we are so focused on executing a plan and the tricky collection of the data that thinking closely about what it might mean gets put off and we won't realize what we saw until we have the chance to reflect and maybe write about it. Either way, the more deeply analytical we are, the more scientific our fieldwork can be, producing work that is focused and fruitful.

Mission-Driven

Ethnographers frequently measure their progress in years. I prefer to replace this expectation with a scale in which one measures one's progress according to the work of a single day. To embrace this standard, one absolutely must embrace the approach Zerubavel proffers. We must not only clarify that in which we are interested before entering the field, however. We must also devise an active and specific plan for how to explore it each day before we go to the field. Such a mission-driven approach to fieldwork supports a more scientific approach because it requires us to pay attention to one specific question for an entire session. The result is a greater likelihood of generating more systematic, rigorous data.

Each day, I suggest that you define a mission for yourself, well before you start trying to take data. Your mission tells you what you're looking for that day. It's the question you want to answer, the task you want to accomplish. Each exercise in this book is an example of one such mission.

The most fruitful missions begin by focusing on the question of *how* things happen—on who, what, where, and when—rather than why. We are attracted to the why question and trained to constantly ask it, but it's a higher-level question. To be systematic, to even begin answering the question of why, one must resist focusing on it. This question can derail any effort at the close observation on which its answer depends. Focus instead on "how" during the day and you'll have your best chance of figuring out "why" later that night.

It can be quite rewarding to set out trying to find something specific and, after an intense day of work, realize you've done exactly that. Ethnographers can get so used to working, working, working, without feeling as if we have much concrete or useful data at the end of a given day, week, month, or year. If we measure our progress only by the number of interviews completed or days spent at our site instead of the number of solid pieces of the puzzle we have fit together, it's a sure sign that we're falling into this pattern.

The opportunity to put on a detective hat and solve one single mystery related to my interests—however small the mystery—is far more appealing than this endless slogging-through-the-mud feeling. First, a mission-directed approach helps me be mindful of what I'm really supposed to be doing. Second, it gives me a solid sense of accomplishment at the end of each day. By focusing on finding specific, factual answers to specific, factual questions, I give myself a satisfying and useful checklist for measuring my progress. Third, being mission-directed helps sustain my energy and enthusiasm over the long term. Daily missions not only remind me of what my goal should be each session, but they also help me accomplish it as each day in the field moves my research relentlessly, enthusiastically forward.

Even if you don't yet know what you're generally interested in, some basic, mission-specific exercises can help you get the lay of the land and find the things that are of interest to you in a quicker, more efficient fashion. Reflecting on the ethnographic enterprise, sociologist Howie Becker (2009, 3–4) argues,

> successful researchers recognize that they begin their work knowing very little about their object of study, and use what they learn from day to day to guide their subsequent decisions about what to observe, who to interview, what to look for, what to ask about. They interpret data as they get it, over periods of months or years, not waiting (in the fashion of a survey analysis, for instance) until they have it all in to start seeing what it means. They make preliminary interpretations, raise the questions those interpretations suggest as crucial tests of those ideas, and return to the field to gather the data that will make those tests possible.

Clearly, fieldworkers operating within this model of a gradual, iterative unfolding of interests, also can reap significant benefits from planning carefully and assigning themselves a small, doable mission for each day in the field.

I see observational and other forms of fieldwork as distributed along a continuum of more and less structured approaches. Fieldwork may be more tightly or loosely structured along at least two dimensions. The first is how well planned a session in the field is and the second is how systematically the data set is collected.

A third, related dimension is how focused or intense you are while collecting data. Analytically, this is a separate matter from how structured the work is. Practically, however, the more structured your approach, the more focused you tend to be while doing fieldwork. A clear agenda for the day enables and promotes a more intense (whether passion-filled or business-like) attitude to getting it done.

Less structured, more softly focused approaches to fieldwork can be beneficial as well. Used in the right combination, both can lead any fieldworker to produce outstanding insights. There are days in the field that I leave wonderfully unstructured, for instance, where I'm tootling around, bumping into people, noticing and reflecting on things that hadn't previously caught my attention. These days are often about getting a sense of the bigger picture and ideas about what to explore further. They also help me get more comfortable and relaxed in the field and increase my chances of striking up new friendships.

But these days feel quite different from the ones when I've carefully planned my mission. With mission-driven sessions I know exactly what I want to have achieved at the end of the day. By then, I'm not only pleasantly exhausted and possibly a bit frustrated, but I also know if I've accomplished what I set out to do. I know what I need to do the next day, too.

Practitioners should have the option to draw from both ends of the spectrum—and all points in-between—as they pursue their individual projects. This is difficult right now, because to my knowledge, few of us have been actively taught how to do ethnography.

There are a number of ways that people typically learn how to do our craft and many ways in which they actually practice it. However, very few of my colleagues have learned from their mentors in a side by side, hands-on fashion. Certainly, when it comes to direct observation, many people have received no formal training in how to do it or what we should expect from it. We end up approaching it in a loosely structured way, equating it with "hanging out and watching" and leaving the results to chance.

When we are too relaxed about what we expect from our fieldwork, it can be difficult to make real progress. It keeps the bar too low for deciding what constitutes a good day's work—or, in the case of PhD students—the work of a good year. In fact, my worry, as a fieldworker and as a teacher, is that for students who are trying to find a foothold and make good progress, the effects of less-than-specific fieldwork can be devastating. Days in the field become weeks, weeks become months, months becoming years. ABDs fall by the wayside. Petitions for extensions are filed with the graduate school. Finally, the graduate student's credit card, family, adviser, and self are equally maxed out. If and when they manage to finish, they may be one of the very few survivors of an unnecessary war of attrition.

If for no other reason than to help future colleagues complete their degrees in much shorter periods of time than were required of previous generations—but without suffering any loss in the quality of their work—we older PhDs must find new, more ambitious, alternative ways of teaching and practicing this incredibly important means of understanding the world. As urban sociologist Richard Ocejo (2013, 4) argues, "learning how to conduct ethnographic research requires not just supervision and practice, but also reflective engagement with its actual practices and strategies. . . . [S]tudents and burgeoning practitioners [must be provided] with examples and models of these practices and strategies to help them think about and conduct their own work." I share this view. I also think that if we can help everyone pick up the pace and the scientific merit of our work while developing better ways of teaching these methods, it would be a very good thing.

One Insight at a Time Can Get You Where You Want to Be
There are lots of ways for a fieldworker to back into valuable insights. I like to take anything I observe and make it into a puzzle, focusing on that question of how. How did this happen? How often does it happen? Is it associated with a specific individual or location, a group of individuals or objects? Is it ever different? Questions like these structure a good part of my time in the field. After a few weeks' effort of such detective work, I definitely have something to show for it.

This intentionally one-day-at-a-time, cumulative approach is like the improvisational comedy game called String of Pearls. In this add-on, storytelling game for up to a dozen people or so, each player helps to build a story by offering a single sentence toward the overall plot. One person starts the story and one person ends it. These two step up and take their places to form the beginning and ending of a line, announcing the story's first and last invented sentences in order. The other players step up one at a time, whenever they want, taking whatever place they want in the line, and randomly fill in the story. By the time the final person joins the line and offers up her/his sentence, an entire story has been pieced together, out of order and one sentence at a time. For a player, the challenge is to pay careful attention to the pieces of the plot already revealed—especially the sentences that come before and after yours—and to offer up a sentence that both makes sense of what's already been said and provides the next piece of the puzzle to move the story toward completion.

String of Pearls is a great way to think of fieldwork. Our job is a little harder because we don't know the last line of the story right from the start. But imagine if each day in the field—each daily mission that you give yourself—produced one sentence, one solid insight that you could state with a confidence. What a story that would add up to at the end of a year! "I may not have the whole picture yet," you say to yourself at the end of a session, "but today, I found out this one thing, for sure. This is definitely one piece of the story I'm trying to construct."

As with String of Pearls, the fieldworkers I know begin building our stories fairly unsystematically, too. Initially, this can be quite freeing. Like String of Pearls players, we have to be especially brave to go first and get things started, but at that point, we can offer up pretty much any sentence—give ourselves pretty much any mission for the day—and get something useful out of it. As the activity continues, however, we start to get a better sense of what's missing from the story we're piecing together. As a result, just like the String of Pearls players who take their turns later in the game, fieldworkers who are farther along in their projects must be much more strategic if their sentences/daily fieldwork are to be as productive as were the earlier contributions.

For fieldworkers, String of Pearls also is a reminder that the solution to any decent mystery is not likely to reveal itself in an orderly, linear sequence. That's how one *tells* the story—later on. It's not how an improv team, police detective, or ethnographer actually constructs it. Rather, we fill in whatever missing pieces we can, a single clue at a time, to solve the mystery. Only then can we tell the story in an organized way.

In sum, if you can set yourself up with a definite question for every day in the field, find a solid, reliable way to get the data you need to answer it, and feel confident in the insight that emerges— you will get where you need to be in the long run. You will have a great story, built up one day, one insight, one sentence, at a time.

This is, incidentally, the way we continue to define and refine our interests as the story/field unfolds itself over the duration of a project. Even if we start with a relatively strong idea of that in which we are interested, the very doing of the research helps us better understand it. The field forms a feedback loop through which we can increase the specificity of our agenda and the intensity of our focus. Gathering and thinking about data allows us to perceive and gather ever-more relevant data as the day—and the project—progresses. This is exactly what Becker alluded to and how we can be ever more creative and systematic as the project matures and we continue to identify what is and is not relevant to our interests. We should think of the process not as a linear sequence of stages, so much as an iterative loop. Like all good design, our daily sessions, as well as our ongoing project, will be defined by this iterative process, as each day helps us discover more of the missing pieces of the story that we want to tell.

On the Scope of the Mission   Critical to building the story one day at a time is the breadth of your mission for any given day. If you bite off too much, it's not necessarily a problem—it just means you'll need multiple sessions in the field before you finally have your answer. Sometimes having to resume the hunt the next day can be quite energizing, making us feel like we're really on to something. As long as you're working hard, the sweeter a delayed discovery can be when you finally make it.

If you bite off too little for a session, it's not necessarily a problem either. You could simply find yourself leaving the field early for the day. Or it might be a signal that you're focusing on too fine a detail, and in the long run, wasting precious time in the field when you could be filling in a bigger piece of the picture. Nonetheless, if you occasionally find that you have given yourself only a smidgeon of a mission for the day, you can always commit to using the rest of your planned time in the field for unstructured observation. Give yourself the chance to think freely and deeply—while dedicating some of that found time to formulating a slightly more substantial question for the next day. It could take some trial and error to figure out what challenge is just right for you. There is no substitute for experience in this regard.

You may find there is an emotional benefit to thinking of ethnographic work as a series of daily exercises. For me, it makes fieldwork a far less intimidating enterprise than thinking of it in its classic, anthropological sense of going to the field each day waiting to see what pops up. Open observation days can feel truly liberating, and I love the freedom to watch with no specific agenda—especially if the result is a number of new ideas for future, well-specified missions. But sometimes those unfocused days make me feel insecure, ungrounded, and overwhelmed—especially if they happen when I'm new to a field or for too many days in a row. Moreover, fieldwork without a specific agenda can leave an ethnographer wondering for weeks or months on end if what they've been doing is of any use.

Instead, fieldwork as a series of focused, daily exercises lets me shift my effort from preparing for a challenge of endurance over the long haul to defining my agenda as best I can, one day at a time, and then going after it, one day at a time. Some days I pay attention to an aspect of my craft—maybe developing a better way to capture something that happens particularly fast or that constitutes an intricately related sequence of behaviors. Some days I focus on what seems to be a taken-for-granted, ever-present behavior, or a suspected pattern that I want to confirm or deny, or maybe an irregular response. Other days, I want to document the dimensions, layout, and flow of traffic in a particular space, or find out what I can learn by paying attention to a particular object for an extended period. Giving myself an assignment like these not only makes each day more doable and my success more apparent, but it also lets me acquire the detailed, systematic knowledge that I find so useful in my work.

Concept-Based

One way to become more analytical and mission-driven in our fieldwork is to let concepts more consciously be our guide. The sociological imagination is certainly anchored in our discipline's concepts. Consciously linking our most powerful concepts to what we look for in the field—and how we look for it—can allow field-workers to generate new, more generalizable theory and analytical frameworks as well as field-specific data. It is a way to pursue a higher-level agenda at the same time that we pursue a local empirical commitment.

Fieldworkers commonly use concepts to organize and make sense of our findings (Becker 1998, 109–145). I believe we use concepts to envision and collect our data too, but on the fly and not nearly as consciously, systematically, or frequently as we might. Here is where our concepts could anchor us far more effectively, if we let them. That is why I intentionally design each exercise, each day in the field, around a specific concept—and why each day in the field requires that you spend time thinking carefully about that concept before you start.

When we first set out to do concept-driven fieldwork, we might discover that our scientific concepts are not as clear-cut and able to be taken for granted as we thought. For a fieldworker, this is a good thing. Ambiguous, amorphous, difficult-to-operationalize concepts allow us to consciously follow and capitalize on the perspective and the strategy articulated so beautifully by the social psychologist Herbert Blumer (1954).

Blumer argues that the field of sociology possesses *sensitizing concepts* rather than definitive ones. Our concepts give us only guidance, he says, rather than precise directions about where and at what we should look.

> Whereas definitive concepts provide prescriptions of what to see, sensitizing concepts merely suggest directions along which to look. The hundreds of our concepts—like culture, institutions, social structure, mores, and personality—are not definitive concepts but are sensitizing in nature. They lack precise reference and have no bench marks that allow a clean-cut identification of a specific instance and of its content. Instead, they rest on a general sense of what is relevant.

As a fieldworker, two aspects of this view of concepts are most attractive to me. First, it leaves room for a fieldworker interested in a specific concept to decide what would be appropriate, relevant data and how they might get it. This view welcomes the researcher's creativity and judgment. Second, by not allowing ourselves to take a concept for granted, fieldworkers can feel free to decide if that concept is actually useful, if others' work using the concept is correct, and if our own work has something new and important to say about it. This view of concepts thus demands a critical approach to our endeavor, bringing additional rigor to it.

As observation-based fieldworkers, we should not limit ourselves to exploring only the concepts most frequently used by other people in our disciplines. Sociologists, for instance, learn that sex, gender, race, and ethnicity, are critically important "master" statuses and experiential lenses in today's world. Whatever methodological approach we favor, much of our work focuses on these concepts. Other, less omnipresent concepts, however, may be uniquely, vitally useful to fieldworkers—especially those of us engaged in direct observation.

When I begin a new project, for example, I draw on two fundamental sociological concepts to start my observations. "Time" and "space" help organize my thinking and provide a failsafe, conceptual entry point. These two concepts and the data I gather to illuminate them provide an essential, baseline understanding of what's going on. I then systematically select from the rest of the concepts in my toolkit to devise other conceptually driven trips to the field. These add onto my base of temporal and spatial findings. Overall, my fieldwork is a direct reflection of the layers of concepts that led to its creation.

Each fieldworker should decide what concepts are most relevant for them and how to design their research around them. Those of us trying to collect observation-based data, however, cannot limit ourselves to the concepts we have most in common with nonfieldworkers, especially when we don't have strong ideas yet for what we might be interested in. Relying on go-to concepts like space and time that may be unique to our interests can be a huge help in taking us somewhere useful and fast, in a wonderfully systematic way. It can also help us understand and refine the concepts that took us there.

Deeply Empirical

More conceptually driven, more scientific fieldwork requires being deeply and unapologetically empirical in how we approach our research. I could not agree more with sociologist John Martin (2011, 321), who argues that sociologists deal in privileged theories, concepts, and accounts of others' behavior and motivations that are rarely challenged by rigorous empirical query. He writes, "This has led to a science in which statements are made about the connection of imaginary elements in an imaginary world, and our justification is the hope that these will explain no case but rather an unknown portion of every case."

My commitment to being as empirical as possible in thinking about theory and concepts came about not only because of my commitment to science and my dissatisfaction with how little raw data I get to see in ethnographic work, but also because of an increasing awareness of my own process as a researcher. Over the course of a project I have a tendency to remember only certain parts of my data—and even those I may not remember quite correctly. Some data points stick out when they happen and therefore stick with me afterward, but there are other data points—and other interpretations of them—that might have passed right by me when they happened. I also tend to preference my growing analysis and explanation over the empirical reality that led me to develop my ideas about it in the first place. What strikes me as "interesting" is not the same across time, either. As I piece things together, I tend to stop paying attention to the pieces of the puzzle that I think I understand, and different things start attracting my attention.

Basically, at any point in the process, my memories of the data threaten to trick me—not because they are wrong, per se, but because they likely are not of the exact, complete information that was previously available to me. As a result, I think carefully about what would be truly useful data and how I can get it in a form that lets me repeatedly revisit it—or fruitfully revisit the field, so I can get new data to check the older data. This allows me to constantly challenge my emerging ideas of what's going on. When I use interview data, I return multiple times to transcriptions of the conversations to double-check that what I think people said is actually, really, truly, what they said. When I use observation data, I do the same, going back repeatedly to the data or the field, to double-check myself. I also try to find ways to re-present and summarize raw data of all kinds that make it easier for me to revisit and reconsider it.

I have learned that I need data that lets me hold my own feet to the fire over the course of a project, and that I must do precisely that. I must resist the urge to let impressions, desires, possibilities, and slippery memories substitute for what really happened. I must try to keep myself relentlessly empirical. What a subject said or did may not be representative of what they actually think or do, overall, but our goal should be to at least respect what they actually said or did at the time and place that we witnessed them doing so. This means we must be not only committed to becoming the best witnesses possible but also to capturing what we witness in the best possible way we can, in a form that will let us revisit the data usefully, over time.

In other words, we should be unapologetically measurement-oriented in our fieldwork. Whenever possible, we should track and quantify what we see as much as what we hear and read. We should look not only for frequencies but also for durations, sequences, and cyclicalities as well as spatial locations and distances between people, objects, and their interactions.

Qualitative researchers should generally make more use of quantified capturings of our fields. Just because we're not afraid to study messy things doesn't mean we have to be messy in how we do it. Being more systematic in how we approach the field—a bit more like archeologists—wouldn't detract from what we do. In fact, it could make it vastly better.

For example, let's say I wanted to study workplace collaboration. I should be interested in more than who said what to whom. I could also pay attention to things like the frequency and duration of interactions, who initiates each interaction, the location (e.g., an office, lunchroom, email, or a voicemail inbox), and the time spent and patterns of exchange in face-to-face versus communication technologically mediated versus document-based interactions. In analyzing these interactions, I could look for patterns such as sequences and cyclicalities as well as patterns that are over- and underrepresented. I could sort the interactions by variables like the organizational unit, hierarchical position, age, race, or sex category of any involved parties—if I gathered that information.

Or I might want to study stranger interactions on the street. To do so, I could eyeball the distances between people walking alone and engaged in civil inattention versus those who appear to be accompanied by another, looking within and outside the bubble of the social unit to see what might be revealed by the amount space between individuals on the sidewalk. I could count the number of times people look at someone else, or touch or talk to each other as well as the duration of each interaction. I could track avoidance maneuvers, from subjects spatially distancing themselves to averting their eyes from each other. I could compare avoidance interactions to interactions meant to invite and encourage more interactions. I could do this for steamy, hot days versus days that are rainy, snow-laden, or sunny. I could collect this data for encounters that happen just before crossing the street versus in front of store windows, private houses, or barren, undeveloped blocks. I could use my imagination, in other words, to come up with and then measure anything that I think might give me more insight on the nature of stranger interactions on the street.

Today's ethnographers are so good at recognizing the value of an anecdote and at taking notes about what seems to matter to people according to the words they say. It can only make our work stronger if we add to this some basic measurements that let us challenge and possibly further support our insights. If we use imaginative metrics to do so, it will be even better.

We would also do ourselves a favor to then present our data in the best way possible. Our standing as social scientists demands that we present our systematic observations to others so that they can independently evaluate their quality and validity. But how often do we present our raw data as well as our conclusions? Usually, fieldworkers give only snippets of quotes, bits of our largely word-based data. Peppered throughout our work, these are more like selective reinforcements of our conclusions, rather than a proper raw data set.

There are often good reasons for this. Editors have assured me that there really is a cut-off for how many pages a book can have before no one will buy it. They have certainly assured me there is a cutoff for how many pages a book can have as a text for classroom adoption. If it comes to a choice between publishing my analysis *or* my data, I know which one I usually pick.

Even if publishers—or clients—are not interested in our raw systematic data, though, we should still have such data. As scientists, we need it to convince ourselves and others of the correctness of our conclusions. Since the time of Galileo and the advent of peer review, scientists have committed to making their raw data available to each other. Our evaluators cannot independently assess the models, interpretations, and insights we offer if they cannot see the data that underlie them. Without it, our readers and audience must take our word for it that what we're saying is right.

I am keenly aware how often I have asked my readers to do exactly this, based merely on whether or not what I'm saying makes sense to them. The coherence of my argument and readers' own experiences and training substitute for access to the data itself. Fortunately, I have engaged in what I believe are good measurements for my claims, even if my data haven't made it into the final product. This reassures me that my conclusions are probably correct— and gives me plenty of extra slides when presenting my work in person.

A more rigorous, scientific approach to our data might make it a bit harder to devalue ethnographic research claims. Our work might be interesting and insightful, ethnography's critics often say, but who knows how reliable it is? More systematically collected and re-presented data would help counter the perception that our work amounts to well-informed opinion rather than carefully obtained findings.

A more systematic, measurement-oriented approach to the visual aspects of our field should also sensitize us to things that our respective disciplines might otherwise encourage us to neglect. Sociologists, for instance, generally neglect the very things that interest designers. Designers typically focus on objects and the built environment, including use and wear patterns, workarounds, forms and materials, and the integration of physical and virtual experience. Objects and the built environment are central to sociology's most fundamental concepts and concerns too, yet we give them a more superficial role in our otherwise incredibly "thick descriptions" (Geertz 1973). Instead, we focus on the institutions, relationships, categories, and codes that define the current sociological lens—the very things designers might find useful yet miss because of *their* training. A more scientific approach will not guarantee that everyone will begin to see everything, or to call it the same thing if they do. But it does increase the possibility of finding and acknowledging the existence of something we might otherwise miss because of the blind spots our training produces.

Creative

To achieve all this, we must not only give ourselves permission to be creative in our fieldwork, we must *expect* creativity from each other. Each of us should expect to take the core knowledge and methods of our disciplines and put our own twist on it. This is how we get new ways of understanding, a greater body of knowledge, and a broader realm of problems to which we can effectively apply both.

The teaching of fieldwork and the results of our fieldwork need to embrace and reflect the essential role of creativity in science. Encouraging creativity is the only way that both the discipline and the individual can be transformed by what each offers to and demands from the other. The result can be work that is not only properly "disciplined" and correct but also fresh and compelling. It is critical that both the teaching and the outcome of fieldwork embrace and reflect the coming together of the disciplinary core and the biographical elements that each individual brings to the process.

Science depends on creativity, in fact, and if we allow space for the different ways different kinds of people have for exploring, understanding, and re-presenting the world, better science will follow. If we are to enter and understand the field as deeply as possible, researchers who are experiential and kinesthetic learners, for instance, may need to encounter the field differently from those gifted in auditory, visual, or writing-based learning. Most people do best when allowed to understand using all modes of learning. Yet we each have some ways of understanding that are more effective for us than others. Similarly, to handicap everyone by only allowing them to express themselves and what they have learned via written words would hardly be sensible. There's a fabulous diversity in what people find interesting and in how we prefer to explore and communicate it. The future of fieldwork as well as our disciplines depends on us embracing this more thoroughly.

Fine arts and studio classes recognize and encourage this relationship between the discipline and the student in wonderful ways. Week after week, the teacher typically issues specific, well-defined problems or challenges and the students respond to them. Students are encouraged to be as creative as they like; the only mandate is that they must meet the challenge given them.

Reality TV shows in which contestants respond to design challenges illustrate the model well. *Project Runway, Cupcake Wars, Face-Off, Iron Chef*—these are all examples of a studio-type class. Each challenger must respond to the same problem and has access to the same materials. Individuals then produce wonderfully different responses. Often, the more well defined the challenges, the more diverse and interesting the outcomes.

I developed the specific, exercise-based approach in this book precisely to encourage creativity in how my students engage and use the field. I aim to help readers maximize their capacity for creativity along a number of dimensions. These include how we: (1) conceptualize and visualize the data that could be most useful to us; (2) collect that data; (3) sort through and analyze this data; and (4) arrange and present our data, our summaries of it, and our conclusions based on it to effectively communicate all of this to others. We should strive to increase our creativity across the ethnographic process, in other words, from what sociologist John Van Maanen (2010, 150–166) calls the "headwork," through the "fieldwork," and the "textwork" phases of our research.

Acquiring and using ethnographic data can be done more or less creatively, of course, including conversational and experiential data. Sociologists Celia Lury and Nina Wakeford (2014, 3–4) offer one of the most recent and interesting reflections on the need for a more creative approach to ethnographic methods in general. The same old thing does not cut it for them, since it does not adequately "enable *the happening* [*sic*] of the social world—its ongoingness, relationality, contingency and sensuousness—to be investigated." Instead, they argue, if we are interested in new problems, experiences, and points of entry, we must invent new methods as well. This is necessary for the simple reason that "it is not possible to apply a method as if it were indifferent or external to the problem it seeks to address."

Here, we explicitly focus only on the acquisition of direct, observational, primarily visual data—not the usual auditory or even participatory data one finds in ethnographic work. Visual data must be captured, analyzed, and often communicated differently from data acquired through interviews, documents, and experiential learning. It calls for diagrams, charts, sketches, and photos. For this reason alone, work produced for these exercises is likely to look different from that which many fieldworkers usually produce, and will challenge and nurture readers' creative sides accordingly.

Why are current ethnographies so word-centric? The question is an interesting one. Anthropologist Anna Grimshaw (2001, 3), for instance, writes about "the curious paradox that other commentators have noted—the centrality of vision to the ethnographic fieldwork developed by Malinowski and his contemporaries, and yet the disappearance of explicit acknowledgment concerning the role of visual techniques and technologies, indeed vision itself, in the new fieldwork-based monograph." This holds true, she argues, despite the fact that "an exploration of anthropology's ways of seeing opens up the questions concerning knowledge, technique and form at the heart of the anthropological project itself" (2001, 172).

Even a cursory examination of sociological ethnographies produces the same conclusion. The lack of visual forms of re-presenting what we observe is a most puzzling counter to the predominance of sight in how so many of us perceive the world today. It leaves us curiously at odds with sensory historian Carolyn Purnell's (forthcoming, 9) summary of what is believed to be a key historical, cultural shift in our sense-making:

The basic narrative of sensory history tends to focus on something called the "Great Divide Theory," which largely comes from the scholarship on orality and literacy pioneered by Walter Ong and Marshall McLuhan. This theory holds that as the world became more literate and print-centered, societies shifted from being "societies of the ear" to being more focused on eyesight. This eye-centeredness supposedly escalated in the eighteenth and nineteenth century, meaning that modernity is characterized by "scopic dominance," or dependence on the eye more than any other sense. Tangled up in this shift were a number of intellectual and perceptual changes. The eye was increasingly seen as the rational, objective sense, *par excellence*, and people put more trust into sight than the other senses.

It's possible that ethnographers' word-centric focus is connected—as both a cause and an outcome—to our neglect of this visual dimension of the field. There are the words spoken then analyzed between people in the field, the words written in a researcher's notebook, the words carefully coded using word-tracking software, and the words the researcher writes in the book based on all these. We ethnographers focus a lot on words, indeed.

My published work can be very word-centric. I love interviewing people and using words—mine and theirs—to describe what they think about what they do. But some of my work also depends on empirical measurements, photographs, sketches, and diagrams to find and support my claims. This work looks (and, I'm happy to say, feels) very creative compared to exclusively text-based work. Even if I do it only for myself, and even if I usually get a clever student to turn my scribbles-in-the-field into a lovely piece of graphic design, it feels well worth the effort.

Just as observation-based data lend themselves to creative work, visual data stimulate and shape our imaginations differently. This is where its longer-term, even transformative power lies. As scientists, we know that concepts, theories, and methods drive our work. They spark our imaginations and help us to see the world—and the field— in a particular way. The resulting lens is what lets individuals look at the same field and see different things. Their imaginations have been cultivated differently and so their mindsets and toolkits take them in different directions. In my field, C. Wright Mills (1959) is well known for his discussion of what we call the "sociological imagination," but others have written at length about the development of scientific thought styles (Fleck 1981), worldviews (Mannheim 1982), paradigms (Kuhn), and mindscapes (Zerubavel 1999).

While you are doing these exercises, let your fieldworker's imagination wander freely, embracing a broad, multimethod approach to envisioning your interests and capturing and re-presenting what you see. Work not only on identifying the key concepts and theories that interest you but also on visualizing what these cognitive constructs might look like in action, in the field. Try to capture that in new ways, using the traditional mental and handwritten notes made while in the field (i.e., what Emerson et.al. (1995) call "headnotes" and "jottings"), and also sketching, photography, videography, and audio recording. Experiment with these more visual ways of capturing and re-presenting data, if you can. Pay attention to your own preferences for each. Think about how you might use each of these tools strategically, in a way that makes sense for you, throughout your process. If you encounter resistance to visual forms of data and re-presentations, try to find a way to respectfully manage that resistance, too, so that your work takes the forms that make the most sense, given the insights you want to convey.

We so rarely get the chance to invert our usual practices and try something new. Enjoy the opportunity to do so. Relish the chance to become a more creative researcher in the process.

Ambitious

When it comes to the way we do our fieldwork, the way we teach it, and the range of problems to which we apply it, we should be unapologetically ambitious. A more rigorous, more focused approach to ethnography might let us do traditional ethnography in more efficient and productive ways, and it could also let us extend its reach to an ever-greater set of problems. Design ethnographers are at the forefront of this movement. Following in their footsteps, fieldworkers everywhere could better participate in solving some of the most pressing challenges we face today if we could work in new ways.

The approach described in this book came about in part because when I think of ethnographers, I not only think of sociologists and anthropologists, but also user-centered designers. User-centered (or human-centered) designers use ethnographic methods to design products, services, systems, buildings, neighborhoods, and even organizational and public policies. As Salvador, Bell, and Anderson (2010) argue, designing effective, socially responsible products requires the kinds of insights that ethnography can uniquely provide, especially in a global context.

Such designers typically work much faster than academics and in teams. They have different concerns from many academic ethnographers, too, focusing more on objects, the built environment, services, and their use patterns. As sociologist Harvey Molotch (2003, 20) argues in his excellent introduction to the world of designers and their impact, by tracing how designers do their work, "one can trace the forces that shape things." Moreover, designers see their work products as deliberately solving existing problems. Indeed, this is environmental psychologist Sally Augustin and interior architect Cindy Coleman's (2012) primary justification for user-centered design research.

Thinking about ethnography as a series of daily missions broadens the contexts in which others also might be tempted to use fieldwork—and the good uses to which we might put it. In general, I am like user-centered designers in that I use ethnographic methods that do not result in traditional ethnographies. Sometimes this is because I am collaborating with designers. But even with my personal, scholarly research, I am less a classic ethnographer than a formal, cognitive, and cultural sociologist who uses ethnographic methods in my work. I do not immerse myself in the lives of a given group of people and then produce detailed accounts of what happened while I spent time with them. Instead, I usually get caught up in a key concept or two and the classificatory schema of which it is a part, then I start looking for the many ways that these cultural, cognitive artifacts are revealed, challenged, maintained, and changed by individuals across multiple social groups.

If we think of ethnographic work only in its classic, deeply immersive, and protracted form—associated with the work of, say, a Margaret Mead—it prevents us from using it in these more analytically focused, applied settings. Ethnographic methods are and will continue to be extremely useful in solving the problems we face. However, to be most useful, the forms in which our methods are practiced—and learned—must continue to evolve. The more ambitious ethnographers can be in envisioning, executing, and teaching our craft, the better we will be able to do our part in helping to meet the challenges around us.

The Well-Tempered Fieldworker

The approach I offer in this book and that underlies each of its exercises reflects my philosophy about the goals to which all ethnographic fieldworkers should aspire. I am not talking about the usual topics of research ethics, the researcher's relationship to the field and the data, or standards of how one gathers and uses one's data. Wonderful sources on these topics already exist. Instead, I focus on the individual researcher's mindset and the matters these exercises were designed to address. This includes how, as fieldworkers, we should approach and envision our job. I believe we should be (a) responsible for ourselves in the field and (b) positive in how we approach our craft—especially when we are trying to improve our ability to do it.

Be Responsible for Yourself in the Field

Director, actor, author, and teacher Mick Napier (2004) is known for his imperative that comedic improvisers should be responsible for themselves, first and foremost. Improvisers should never have to rely on another player's "gift" in order to get the scene started. The same is true for every fieldworker

First, we should aspire to never having to rely on anyone else to tell us what to do in order to get started on any given day in the field. We should have our own ideas of what might be useful to know and how we might find it out, well before we start taking data. Just as in improv, some of what we start with will drop out, strengthen, or morph into other things as the day continues. But we should start with a specific, doable plan of some sort if we are to begin with any measure of confidence. If we are working on a team, of course we should confer with others about our ideas for the day. However, we shouldn't have to do so to get started and have something to show for it later on.

Second, we should be the strongest, most agile, and versatile fieldworkers possible. This includes developing a diverse set of skills and practices that we can draw on as needed. We must aim to be the best at both conceptualizing and acquiring our kind of data. We must also strive to be the best storytellers in the room, able to represent that data, our insights, and our conclusions in ways that are accurate, persuasive, and tailored to the audiences at hand. We must commit to exploring our fields deeply, in other words, and always be open to new ways to do this.

... and a Positive Presence

Doing any of this requires that we be positive in how we approach our roles as learners, practitioners, and, if we have the chance to work with other fieldworkers, teammates. Fieldwork should be an engaging, enjoyable, and affirming activity. If it's not, we're sabotaging ourselves. We should note frustration points and moments of negativity so that we learn from them—but we should not dwell on them.

It's vital for readers to follow this principle throughout this book. If you get stuck and can't seem to progress as you tackle each of these exercises, change things up to break out of the mental rut and your less-than-useful focus on it. Make your work fun again. Getting distraught over one's fieldwork can lock your brain onto the points of frustration and the condition of being stuck. This alone can prevent you from being successful.

Most important, always remember to note what worked well for you. It's easy to hear the self-critic inside. Drown it out by making a conscious effort to hone in on the victories at the end of the day—especially the little ones. Raise the things you did well to a level of awareness that outshines any tendency you might have to focus on the ones that didn't go so well. This is a key to resiliency, one of the most important traits we should deliberately work to develop in ourselves.

Above all, remember that fieldwork is a set of learned behaviors, skills, and judgment. Success or failure in the field is rarely about you as a person. It is about where you are in the process of becoming an ever-better fieldworker. If it doesn't go well one day, lighten up, start again from different angle, and allow yourself to learn.

If you do, then you will be in fantastic shape for working with others. It is common for ethnographers to work in small groups today. This works best if each individual is a well-trained, forward-thinking, positive presence for themselves and anyone else. The better you are as an individual fieldworker, the more easily you'll be able to offer up important gifts to teammates, too. No matter how much you like working on your own, the joy and unexpected, synergistic outcomes of working with a group of strong, creative fieldworkers is not to be missed.

My perspective on fieldwork is the foundation for the exercises and discussions in this book. As we now turn to those exercises, I will discuss the issues raised here in more depth. Before heading to the field for Exercise 1, however, you will want to gather a few things. Eventually, you will no doubt adjust what is in your personal fieldworker's kit, but these items should get you started.

Packing List

The following items will help you do the exercises in this book with minimal distractions:

1. You'll need a way to take notes. For most people this means a sturdy notebook and writing implements. The notebook should have hard covers and it should open and fold back on itself so it lies flat and can be easily written in while standing. Spiral-bound is best for this. Not too big and not too small for you and the size of your hands and forearms. You'll also want a pen and pencil that are easy for you to use and that make it easy to decipher what you wrote later on.

Your note-taking tools are a matter of fit with each other as well as with you. You need writing implements that work well for you on the particular notebook that you select. These writing tools might be different from what you normally use on other paper and under different writing conditions. Some pens are scratchier, move more slowly, and leave messy blots on some kinds of papers. Some pens have ink that bleeds through some papers and can make it hard to use both sides of a page. Different pens need to be held differently for the ink to flow freely. You'll be standing much of the time, resting your hand only on your notebook as you write, so this may also affect the type of pen you choose. Softer lead pencils move across the page more easily but they may need sharpening often and the graphite can smudge over time. The lead in mechanical pencils can break easily in the throes of taking field notes. You will rely greatly on your notebook's legibility and your speed and comfort while writing in it so some experimentation is worth your while. Even if you normally prefer to take notes on a digital device, you will probably find analog options are better in this instance.

2. You also will need a way to keep track of time. You'll need a watch with a second hand or, even better, if you have it, a cell phone with a stopwatch/interval app and possibly headphones.

3. You may want to take photos. If you have access to a camera, whether on your cell phone, iPad, or a single lens reflex (SLR), bring it with you to the field.

4. Your fieldworker's kit also should acknowledge your physical needs. Include water, easy-to-eat snacks, cough drops, tissues, and whatever else might help keep you comfortable. Use the restroom before you start a session. No one wants to have to interrupt data-taking to take care of such an easily predictable need.

5. If you bring a phone—and it's a good idea in case of emergency—silence it. Make it a policy to work without interruption. It's not a caller's fault if they wreck your flow by calling; they can't see how hard you're working. Head them off at the pass and impose this discipline of inaccessibility on all potential callers. Also, do not allow yourself the distraction of calling someone if you get frustrated or tired. These sessions are only one hour long. They help you to build concentration at the same time that they require it.

6. Unlike fieldwork focused on interviewing, observation work means you often have to move to get your data. You want to be self-contained, hands-free, and efficient in your movements, able to easily access any of your tools at any time. You'll want a back-

pack or carryall that makes it easy to secure your things in a public place without having to be overly mindful of them.

7. You will need a site for your fieldwork, keeping in mind all the elements discussed so far. Be sure that your field site is open and accessible to you on the dates and times you plan to work.

8. Finally, each time you go to the field, you may wish to bring this book with you. It might be useful to reread the prediscussion and the assigned exercise right before you get started.

Part Two: The Exercises

Exercise One—
Open Observation

There is no prediscussion for this exercise. Just get started.

Select a group of individuals to watch within your chosen field site. Observe your subjects for one hour. Take notes on what you see in whatever way makes sense to you. Write up your notes in two to five pages, reporting on your observations. Pretend the report is for me or some other person—not just yourself. Do this write-up also in whatever way makes sense to you. Scan your field notes and attach them to your report.

Please do not read further until you have completed this exercise, including the report based on your fieldwork.

silverback

birth

3/11/91   Kivan (M) - large. gray hair on back, loose torso. moderately active.
1/9/79   Kowali (F) - medium, but large, round belly. MIA.
4/20/96   Mahiri (F) - medium. folded ears. moderately active.
1/22/89   Balara (F) - medium. lethargic. loner.
7/26/05   Amare (M) - small. playful + restless.

To make matters worse, I initially did not know any of the gorillas' names, making it considerably harder to take notes and distinguish one from another...

Post-Exercise Discussion

For some people, this is the book's hardest exercise. It's worth the effort. In the best tradition of John Dewey, there's nothing like learning by doing. I haven't found a better way to focus attention on the challenges that lie at the heart of fieldwork.

Let's look at what's involved in an exercise like this. On the spot, possibly while watching a species you knew nothing about, you had to come up with (1) your own agenda for the session and (2) your own way of trying to achieve that agenda, including (3) a way to capture what you saw. Afterward, you also had to come up with (4) a way to write it all up.

The clarity and appropriateness of these decisions is precisely what determines the quality of one's fieldwork. Newcomers may have moments of trepidation because of how immediately apparent and unavoidable these decisions are during and after their time in the field. What do I pay attention to? How do I keep track of what I see? How should I summarize this? If you experienced multiple moments of hesitation in deciding how to forge ahead on any of these questions, that is excellent. Awareness of the decisions we have to make is critical to successful fieldwork.

Imagine if you had a plan along all these lines *before* you started your session. For the rest of this book, you will be preparing yourself to do exactly that—to come up with a good plan for what to do each time you go to the field and for what to do afterward, when you are processing and writing up what you've seen. By the time you finish all the exercises, you should be better able to (1) envision a daily agenda and a creative way of operationalizing it; (2) get the kind of data you desire; and (3) effectively write up (or, better, re-present) and communicate your findings to others.

Of all the questions and decisions in this first exercise, the most important is the decision about what you will pay attention to when you're in the field. Everything depends upon and flows from the clarity of your daily scholarly agenda—your specific conceptual and analytic interests drive the mission you give yourself as you operationalize and collect data related to them. You can have extraordinary technical skills as a fieldworker but without an agenda driving the use of those skills, it is difficult (if not impossible) to get meaningful data from your time in the field. The lack of agenda is why students commonly feel a bit lost with this exercise, unsure what they should have focused on or if what they got was in any way useful or "right." You would not be able to make progress toward a larger, compelling whole if you continued this way.

This is the "garbage in, garbage out" lesson for fieldworkers. The quality of what we get out of the field on any given day is a function of what we put into it before our fieldwork starts. Planning the day is everything. Fieldworkers have to be creative and flexible and able to change their plans on the fly. But the more thought we put into each session in the field—the better our plans are to begin with—the more easily we'll be able to adapt and even change those plans altogether. You'll still have something tangible to show for it afterward too. This is how one makes progress as a fieldworker, one productive day at a time.

Perhaps the biggest concern that emerges from this first exercise—especially for novice fieldworkers—has to do with field notes. This concern centers on a variety of related questions. What are field notes? How do they function? How do we take them? What are the different forms in which they might be taken, including photographs, sketching, or filling in data templates? What is the difference between data and other note-worthy elements? How might we keep track of immediate versus longer-term interests? How long we should watch versus record what we see? How many notes should we take? To these, I add one more: what do our field notes reveal about us and our development as field-workers?

The rest of this discussion is dedicated to these important questions. Novice fieldworkers tend to worry nicely about their field notes. More experienced researchers may have to work to see and possibly reconsider all the decisions they've already made in how they handle their notes. Whichever you are, I encourage you to spend time reflecting on your field notes from this point forward.

Let's start by considering the definition of "field notes." The term commonly refers to two different but related sets of notes. The first set of notes is what Emerson, Fretz, and Shaw (1995) call "jottings." These are the scribbles we make in real time, during our observation sessions. The second set of notes—what Emerson and colleagues call "field notes"—is a more cohesive write-up of one's jottings. It is written as soon as possible after completing a session in the field, to flesh out the more cryptic jottings as accurately as possible.

I differ from Emerson and colleagues in that I use the term "field notes" to refer to "jottings"—our scribbled, notes-in-the-field, taken in the heat of battle. For me, these are the quintessential "field notes." Whenever I use the term "field notes" throughout the rest of this book I am referring to those jottings, our original capturings taken in real time while *in* the field.

I refer to the more complete expansion of in-the-field-notes that fieldworkers typically produce later on as your "write-up" or "written-up field notes." We will not discuss them at length, as others already do a great job of that, and I will not ask you to produce this second set of notes although you may wish to do so.[1] Instead, for each exercise, I'll ask you to write a report on what you did while in the field and what you learned from it. This report often incorporates a fleshed-out version of a student's scribbles-in-the-field, but not always. It will depend on the exercise and your reporting style. Some students present data summaries only, while others include a fully written-up version of their entire session in the field. Do whatever you find useful.

This report encourages you to think of your trips to the field as a series of pedagogical, self-reflective sessions. In writing each report, you will no doubt turn some of your field notes into more complete, narrative summaries. However, you probably won't expand on everything, creating fully transcribed and carefully detailed versions of your field notes in the ways fieldworkers normally do. For our purposes, it's not necessary. It's more important to spend your time thinking about your overall process as a fieldworker.

For many researchers, field notes are composed of almost entirely words. You should not limit yourself in this way. Observation data should include visual note-taking like quick sketches, no-fuss photographs, rough-hewn diagrams, and other methods that let us better capture data and context and help us recall it later. These can be highly effective methods/tools for communicating one's findings to others as well.

In fact, field notes serve at least three functions. Their most obvious and straightforward purpose is as mnemonic devices. Your notes are re-presentations of your data, your interpretations of your data, and anything else that happened while you were in the field that you found noteworthy. Your notes help you reconstruct your in-the-field experience.

Field notes can serve a second purpose as well. Since they are the closest capturings we have of our data, some people reference their field notes in formal arguments to validate their conclusions. Just as a physicist might show a graph of the data collected in an x-ray scan to justify her conclusions, an ethnographer might include an excerpt from his field notes—a chart, a quote, a photograph or sketch—to do the same.

In these exercises, your field notes will serve a third purpose. They will function as a critical diagnostic tool, helping you develop a better understanding of yourself as a fieldworker. Over time, your field notes can offer a remarkable window into your transformation as an observer, recorder, sense-maker, and storyteller. We can use them to trace our journeys as fieldworkers.

This connects to another cluster of concerns for researchers new to field notes, centered on the issue of for whom our scribbled-in-the-field notes are written. Field notes exist primarily to serve your purposes and yours alone. It is up to you if you decide to show them to anyone else. The beginning of a process through which we capture and begin to make sense of what we observe, our field notes should consist of the quickest, most accurate ways to capture information so that we can easily recall it when we finally sit down and engage it more fully.

Given our different skill levels, this means that different information may be best captured through different forms of re-presentation. If the fastest, most accurate way for you to capture something is to sketch it, then do that. Sometimes, a single photograph will jog your memory most effectively.

If you're lucky enough to be multilingual, then you might find that some observations are most quickly and accurately tagged through one language, others through a different one. Don't hesitate to use whichever language works best for you in your note-taking. You can put everything in one language during your write-up. Let your field notes be tailor-made for you.

Do whatever works to help you capture information in the field. But remember to give yourself opportunities, like these exercises, to practice taking data in ways that challenge you. Plan sessions in the field when the data do not count so you can practice newer ways of capturing it. Acquire as big and diverse a toolkit as you can for getting the job done.

Many fieldworkers don't draw, for instance. Some can be resistant to trying. If, however, you're sitting in the field, doing one of these exercises, and you find yourself thinking, "Darn it! I wish I could draw!" then do so, right then and there. It doesn't matter if, say, your hasty gorilla sketch looks like the symbol pi or if your painstaking, one-hour-long line drawing looks like a mutant from a Godzilla movie. Either that pi symbol will capture something for you far more effectively than words could, or it won't. You'll either learn something unique about that gorilla from the process of drawing your mutant, or you won't. You have nothing to lose from trying.

No one else has to see your experimental scribbles, sketches, or lousy photos. No one else has to see the heavy underlining, the multiple question or exclamation marks, or all the stars you used to signal your internal dialog. Your excited commentaries, "Did I really just see what I thought I did?!" or "Holy Cow! This is really important!," are only for you. No one else has to see your honest brackets with nothing but a question mark between them, either—or however you indicate to yourself that you didn't see what happened just then. If you try something new in your note-taking and it doesn't work, then you've learned that you need to try a different approach— or to practice more. And you'll have already started to do both.

The most vital elements for you to focus on are the data and any important contextual constraints you had in getting it. Most fieldworkers also want to keep track of anything that strikes them as interesting or important while collecting their data. Add anything else you wish to your notes, as long as you clearly distinguish between what you observed and whatever else you write down. It's the data you should be interested in, first and foremost.

What, exactly, is your data? Your data consist of the actual things you observe, including the time and place in which they happen. Your data may be captured in many forms, recorded strictly in the field, or fleshed out in stages when you have time to elaborate. The important point is to always remember that your data are what happened, and when and where it did so. Anything else is something else. It is not data.

Because we often strive to capture the fullness of our experience in our field notes, they often include a variety of contextual elements like thoughts about what just happened, questions about the meaning of something we saw, ideas for the data we'd like to get next—all kinds of musings. These notes can be hugely relevant to our work. They can be the whole point of taking data (as in, sudden realizations because of what we just saw.) But for the purposes of this book's approach to observation-based research, feelings, impressions, interpretations, and contextual matters do not constitute "data." In fact, one of your goals should be to get better and better at recognizing the difference between what actually just happened and your interpretations and applications of it. The ability to separate data from reaction is what brilliant careers in science—natural, social, behavioral, and all the professions to which they have given birth—are founded on.

This is why it is so important that you develop a system to keep these things separate from and subordinated to the acquisition of data—both in your notes and in your mind. All of these other matters provide important details and insights to help you interpret the data and tell your story later. While they can be the end goal of your mission, your primary focus should be getting the raw data and keeping it separate from these other elements, so you avoid confusing what actually happened with your interpretations and uses of it.

This view of one's experience in the field and what appears in one's notes requires many of my students to do a gestalt trick. Many students tend to prioritize their thoughts about what they see, over careful descriptions of what, exactly, they saw. Initially, their notebooks are filled with detailed reflections on what they observed but not much about what actually took place. There may be lots of close thinking, which is good, but the field is too incidental to the process.

There is an easy fix for this problem. Simply make the data your primary reason for being in the field. Let all your thoughts *about* the data fall into place behind, alongside, and otherwise separated from it. It helps to develop a visual mechanism in your notes for keeping track of the difference between something observed and your thoughts about it. This is a matter of good scientific practice.

Again, the thought can be a question about what an observed fact means. It can be a reflection about how what you just saw relates to something observed at another time. It can be a postulation about what might have happened while your view was blocked and you could not see the subject. Whatever the thought is, find a way to demarcate that for yourself, so that when you look at your notes it is instantly clear whether a given note is about something that you actually saw or about something you thought. Write your thought as a question. Put it in brackets. Underline it. Whatever technique you choose, you need a personal convention so you can clearly, visibly differentiate what you have seen in the field from your thoughts about it. This, alone, will help you become a more disciplined, scientific observer, able to better separate empirical reality from your interpretations of it.

What should you take notes about? Whether words or line drawings or anything else, the point of field notes is to quickly capture what seems significant to you while it's happening. These notes are gold no matter how messy and cryptic. They will help you recall moments and details that might elude you otherwise. They serve as placeholders, keeping a spot in your memory warm until you can sit down and make fuller sense of what you saw.

This is why your scholarly agenda and your mission for the day are so important. They help you decide what is significant. If something you see is related in any way to your mission for the day, then it is data and you should make note of it. You don't have to understand why it seems significant—you can always figure that out later. Trust your gut. Intuition is a fieldworker's best friend. The feeling that something may be related to what you're interested in can be based on previous experience and/or a connection you're making of which you are not even aware. That feeling should not be dismissed. You'll develop more confidence in your ability to identify data as you gain experience and expertise. This is one of the signs of being an authority on something—having a good sense of what is and isn't relevant to a problem at hand—and being able to articulate why.

Don't forget to note the things that seem normal, commonplace, predictable, and, well, boring. Part of the trick of good fieldwork is learning to be as excited by the everyday and taken for granted as we are by the special, the novel, and the new. It is the element of cognitive salience to our scholarly agendas that determines what goes in our notes, not the element of exoticism. No detail is too small, no interaction, too routine. As long as something seems relevant to your mission for the day, it should be in your notes. Your challenge is to see the mundane as the exciting discovery it can be.

Another hallmark of an outstanding fieldworker is one who is simultaneously immersed in the specifics of a particular field on a given day while also being aware of and looking for more general patterns of behavior. Every session should be seen as a potential touchstone that can inform our larger, possibly career-long questions and interests. Again, the trick is to find a way to clearly, easily keep larger themes and interests separate in your notes from your data and your mission for the day. The judicious use of highlighters in your notes and the creation of theme-driven, synthetic documents to which you add excerpts over time also might help you identify and weave themes and interests across different projects.

This first exercise may have introduced you to another core concern about field notes: How do you figure out how much to watch and how much to write while you're in the field? Specifically, this is the issue of the duration of each activity as you switch back and forth between them. We typically may only watch *or* document what we see. Many students start this course believing that they watch and take notes "at the same time." This is only possible, however, when we are making the most minimal of notes, perhaps blindly scribbling numbers onto a table in our notebooks while literally not taking our eyes off our subjects. Mostly, students who describe themselves as watching and writing "at the same time" are actually alternating very rapidly between these activities, in an irregular fashion.

For observational fieldwork, you should generally watch as long as you can while still being able to comfortably document what you've just seen. Document what you saw as quickly as you can, too, so that you can resume observing as soon as possible. The basic problem is this: if you watch for too long, you'll forget important details or sequences by the time you start—and eventually finish—writing it down. You'll also forgo watching new things for a longer period, because you'll be busy writing down the older stuff. If you watch too little, you may not see important details, a whole sequence, or vital contextual information that would shed important light on your little snippet of action.

This means that the duration of our observation time and note-taking times will vary across a given session as well as across different sessions in the field. Sometimes there's an awful lot going on at once. Sometimes it's a slow day. Sometimes you can't keep up with what you'd normally manage because you're under the weather or distracted. Change the amount of time you watch and the amount of time you write as needed.

Experiment to find a good balance between the length of your observation and writing periods. This book includes exercises based on interval research, in part to draw your attention to this important aspect of fieldwork. I strongly suggest that you begin by consciously separating your observation periods from your note-taking periods, observing for short, frequent durations. Shorter observation periods are more memory-friendly. They also let you more quickly note what happened then return your attention to the action. More frequent data points are generally better for capturing the sustained thread of the action, too. This approach is also less likely to result in frustration and generic, glossed-over data that lacks specifics.

This principle applies to note-taking in any media. However, the time it takes to document what is going on varies across all the forms of note-taking we might use, and each has trade-offs. For instance, photography is a super-fast way to record what you see. With current low-to-mid-priced DSLR cameras, one can easily capture hundreds of images in an hour. This might seem a wonderful option for fieldworkers worried about missing things while writing them down. However, for most researchers, such an approach results in an overwhelming amount of superfluous data and, while taking all these photos, it is virtually impossible to mentally process any of what is going on. You would have to push off all the analysis—the most important part of our work—to a later time, when you could go through and think about each photo. Unless all the shots captured essential information that you wanted to carefully code for a time series study, it would be much better to take photos selectively and sparingly, using the time in the field to encounter, explore, and think about what you're seeing.

A number of fieldworkers rely on lengthy, sometimes automatic video recordings of what happens in their research site in lieu of selective documentation in real time. This results in the same problem. Actually watching and analyzing what's going on gets pushed off to another time, if it happens at all. When researchers

do look at it later, they stare at a screen to do so instead of observing in real time at the actual location.

I find that looking through the viewfinder of any type of camera severely limits my natural field of view and alters my experience in the field. When photographs are essential, I prefer to work as part of a team. Design ethnographer and gifted photographer John Dominski and I work this way. For analytical photography, two sets of eyes are much better than one, especially if one set has a full, unencumbered field of view and the other stays focused on capturing the world through the lens.

Unlike photography, one needs a substantial amount of time to visually capture what one observes with a careful line drawing. The subject may very well move before the drawing is complete. Just as with photographic and video imagery, one must balance the trade-offs, and be strategic in when and how one uses the advantages of a sustained drawing for capturing data and insights. If the subject is sleeping, or sitting at a desk for a prolonged period, for instance, one might be able to minimize the amount of data and insights one must forgo while producing the drawing. One could also rely on fast sketches whenever possible rather than painstaking, detailed drawings.

There is one more aspect to the question of "how much should I write?" People have very different ways of taking handwritten notes, from the amount of notes we take to the forms in which they appear. Some researchers are parsimonious, with notes that look more like spare lists of keywords—possibly in multiple languages—and partially drawn cartoons. Some produce ways of quickly recording and summarizing what they see via tables, charts, and other templates that let them write very few words. And then there are researchers who produce the equivalent of a Victorian journal with fully formed and grammatically correct sentences that go on for pages.

Wherever you fall on a long list of diverse options, remember: you should have enough recorded in your notes so that when you write up your report for the day's exercise, you can do it without being frustrated. Take enough notes so you can remember exactly what happened. The task at hand, the nature of the field, how well you pay attention, and how well your memory works will all influence how much you need to do this.

This brings me back to the diagnostic function of your field notes. As you proceed with these exercises, try to look at your field notes in a curious, dispassionate way. They can help you discover how you think, how you work, your fallback assumptions and techniques, and the edges of your comfort zone. They can show where you are in your journey as a fieldworker—even a particular *kind* of fieldworker, trained in a certain discipline or profession— and how you have changed over time. Your field notes can be a remarkable tool for self-discovery.

When you look at what you did for this first exercise, for instance, what do your field notes reveal about what you were drawn to—and possibly why? If your notes seem wildly out of sync with what you would normally find fascinating in this situation, remember to give yourself permission to pursue what *you* find interesting in the way that you do so. We often start off trying to second-guess and fulfill others' expectations. However, if your goal is to do field-work in a more innovative and potentially effective way than your teachers (including yours truly), you'll need to absorb and learn everything you can from them and then move beyond it. We should incorporate others' expectations to surpass them. Follow your own nose in deciding what path to follow—or what trail to blaze.

In that vein, when you look at your notes, can you tell what your personal goals were for the observation session? Was it simply to get a feel for what's going on? Was it to collect systematic data of some kind? Do your notes reveal anything about what you can handle in terms of the observational venue or challenge you selected for yourself, as opposed to one you might try in the future? Keep in mind that you may need to select a different field site, given your goals, if you continue to feel frustrated by a possible mismatch.

Your notes may also reveal if you're struggling to find the right balance between watching and note-taking. They may provide clues about how comfortable you are in relying on memory alone for details—and how hard-pressed you might be to convince others of what you saw because of it. As you write your reports, keep an eye out for the possibility that you are trying to remember too much, relying on notes that are too few. If that's the case, decrease the duration of your watching and give yourself more time to write up what you just saw.

Overall, when you look at your field notes, what kinds of collecting, recording, and re-presenting skills could you add to your current bag of tricks to strengthen what you already do well? Start by cataloging the choices you see for how you recorded what you saw. Did you use only words or did you use more visual forms of note-taking too? Did you use any digital technologies, collecting visual or auditory information via some device? What do you learn by comparing the techniques—and possibly languages—you used to capture what you were seeing? Are some more effective for you in certain situations than others? The choices that multilinguists make in their field notes are fascinating, often seeming to reflect the language used when the individual first learned about a concept or action—sometimes the mother tongue, sometimes the language spoken at a school of higher education.

What do you learn by comparing the techniques you used to *capture* data with those you used to *communicate* it to others? It's not just the difference between these modes of communication that are interesting; it's also whether or not there is a cost to giving up what you did in your note-taking phase when you moved into the report-writing phase. Do you think you gained or lost anything in the translation process as you fleshed out and typed up—perhaps even computer modeled—your findings? Nuances captured in our scribbles and our messy sketches may be lost when we turn them into nice, tidy computer renderings, although these cleaned up, digital versions may well allow us to better communicate our intentions to others.

Was there anything that, in hindsight, you didn't notice or make a record of while you were in the field that you regretted later on? It's as important to note how you react to and treat information when you discover it's missing as how you respond to it when it's present. If you realized something was missing, what was your reaction? Did you try to reconstruct the information another way? To fudge it over and either ignore its absence in your write-up or make up something plausible to fill the gap? Did you decide simply to remember the frustration and dedicate yourself to getting what was missing next time? The last is your best choice. I would far rather see a student's notebook with a page dotted with blanks and question marks than with feasible but made-up claims and camouflaged suppositions. If you do fill in any blanks with things that you did not directly witness but seem plausible, be clear that's what they are. Your best guess can be really important sometimes, as long as you indicate that's what it was.

One very simple thing that affects what we see and what we miss is our field of view. Did you include your location and position in your notes? If you are close to your subjects, you will be able to see facial expressions, nuances of body language, and micro-elements of *how* certain things are done—but only by one or two individuals, perhaps. If you are farther away, you might be able to see overall patterns of movement and activity among a larger group and area of space. Comings and goings are best seen with a wider lens, and you might notice these matters by sitting farther away from your subjects. Did you find yourself changing your viewpoint during your session and did the things you were interested in, or the ways you addressed them, change accordingly? Do not forget to make a note whenever you shift your viewpoint. This, too, will help you make sense of your data as well as what you are drawn to at different times.

Whatever you did for this first exercise, you might think of it as a baseline in how you capture and share what you've seen—possibly a starting point for a stronger, more complete fieldworker's toolkit in the not-too-distant future. As you progress through these exercises, respond to them freely, meeting each challenge with as much creativity as you can. It will not do the body of scientific knowledge much good if all we do is keep cloning ourselves. This is fine for passing on canonical knowledge and ways of thinking. It's not so great for generating new content, new methods, and new approaches.

Take one more look over your report for Exercise 1. Now, pay special attention to the things you did well. I do not expect anyone to do any of the following in this first exercise. However, it's a very good sign if your report included:

- Some contextual information, including details like where you were, what was going on around you, the time, the temperature, the feel of the place, how many subjects you observed, who and where they were, and so forth
- The time that something happened
- The duration of an activity
- Any other kind of measurement
- Descriptive details of the environment and the objects found in it

- *How* something happened, not just what, generically, it was
- Information conveyed via a sketch, diagram, or photograph instead of words
- Mention of something that changed for you, as an observer, and that affected your ability to watch what was happening
- A time you took a guess at what was going on—and indicated that it was a guess
- A question for yourself, clearly indicated as such
- An observation about yourself, and your process, as a field-worker
- A differentiation between your raw notes and what you might have added to them later on, while writing your report (e.g., this could be as simple as including scanned copies of the raw field notes with your report or, in the report itself, using different fonts or colors, etc., to indicate what was a raw note and what was additional material, added afterward)
- An indication that you recognized that you had attributed a motive or emotion to a subject without really knowing if that's what she or he thinks/feels

The rest of the exercises will give you tasks that are much more specific, becoming more difficult as they proceed. I'll address the conceptual, mechanical, and communication challenges associated with each to systematically develop your sophistication in all these parts of the fieldwork process. I hope the exercises will not only help you develop some new skills but also to convince you why a more directed, well-planned, and focused mission for each day in the field can be so useful for any fieldworker.

You may now wish to take a look at some sample responses to this exercise produced by my previous students. Along with a few brief comments about each response, you will find their responses at http://global.oup.com/us/watchingclosely.

Note

1. In general, the reason you normally would take the time to write up your field notes is that weeks or months down the road, you will be much better able to remember what happened on any given day if you read the second, "written-up" set of notes than if you looked at your original scribbles. If we are working on teams and have agreed to share our daily insights from the field, this written-up, fleshed-out version of our notes is often mandatory. Our field notes are unlikely to make sense to anyone else on the team.

Exercise Two—
Temporal Mapping I

This exercise directs your attention to the temporal dimension in fieldwork—how temporal structures infuse observed behavior and how attending to time can enhance the quality and versatility of the data one collects. I will ask you to make consistent note of the time that your observations occur as well as reflect on the ways natural and artificial temporal structures pervade what you see. Exercise 3 builds on the sensitivities and skills that you begin to develop here.

A large part of the challenge posed by the first exercise stemmed from the lack of a specific, focused agenda. Of course, you eventually settled on an agenda for yourself, although it probably was not as clear or useful as it could have been if you thought about it beforehand. As a result, like the sample responses to that exercise posted online, your report was probably an overview of what you were looking at—possibly describing some physical attributes of your subject, certain aspects of the environment, some of the interactions you saw, and maybe what seemed to be going on whenever you noticed a new individual or a change in the action. This kind of mash-up is what usually results when we don't have a specific agenda, culled from field notes that are random bits of everything that we think might be important—even if we're not sure how or why.

This is a normal approach to fieldwork and to a first day in the field. However, this time, we are going to embark on a well-planned session driven by a clear mission for the day. Giving yourself a well-structured assignment for the day can be critical if one wishes to make tangible progress. Whether you want to improve an aspect of your craft or gain particular information about the field, taking the time to decide what, specifically, you want to accomplish that day is essential. It gives you a clear mental starting place and a way of deciding if you've accomplished what you set out to do.

A structured way of writing up what you've learned is equally helpful. It not only helps document and communicate what you've learned, but it also sensitizes you to what you should be doing in the first place. If you know what you want to produce from the observation work, it helps you know what to do during your field-work. Hence, this next exercise will give you a good scholarly agenda for a day in the field and a good, single day's mission based on that agenda. I'll also give you a very simple format for writing up your report.

When I enter the field—no matter what my scholarly agenda is for the project overall—I start with two questions: What's happening here across time? What's happening here across space? Time and space are always at the top of my list of sensitizing concepts. Focusing on these helps me quickly make sense of what I'm seeing.

Accordingly, these next two exercises are on time and the two after that are on space. Even if you don't have any idea what else you should attend to, this is a great starting point for any fieldworker, for any project. I may spend the first couple weeks of any project doing these exercises over and over, by selecting a different focal point, time of day, day of week, location, or social unit for each session. I also scatter repeats of these exercises throughout the full duration of my fieldwork. This is designed to keep me checking myself against the data as I start to develop ideas and conclusions.

I start with time because, between time and space, time seems to be most fieldworkers' weaker hand. We tend to ignore the value of time's structural dimensions and their profound impact on social organization and individual behavior. One can achieve a marked elevation in the usefulness of observation work simply by paying more attention to this aspect of social life.

Throughout these exercises I offer a distinctly sociological approach to thinking about time and space. There are other approaches to these concepts. You should draw from those too and develop your own ideas of these concepts so they can enhance fieldwork in a way that will be unique to you. For now, I'll provide some basic ways to think about time to help you along.

Temporal Structures—Natural v. Artificial

Natural time—so far as we know—is a continuous phenomenon. It is most obviously demarcated for us by change in our position relative to the sun. Days, nights, seasons—these visible changes show what is natural along the temporal dimension. Species develop signature behaviors around these natural temporal structures, like diurnal and nocturnal patterns of activity, or specific eating and vocalization habits that occur at different times of the day—or year. Seasonal behaviors among plant and animal species include annual reproductive and maturation cycles, as well as activities like migration, hibernation, and changes in fur and feathers associated with the time of year.

As social beings, we add a layer of artificial temporal structures and behaviors over the natural elements of time. We minimize our awareness of and adjustment to natural time with a focus on our own fabricated times, like the school day, Memorial Day, rush hour, the workweek, vacation, the fiscal quarter, and our yearly religious and secular holiday calendars. Artificial temporality may be rooted in the 24-hour day and the 365.25-day year that nature gives us, but it can subordinate temporality's natural roots and make it fairly irrelevant to our daily lives.

If natural time is linear, then artificial time is about patterns of repetition layered over it. Sociologist Eviatar Zerubavel's *Seven Day Circle* makes this point beautifully. Tracing the history of the week, this work serves as an essential introduction to artificial versus natural time as well as the consequences of standardized sociotemporal structures. Zerubavel argues that the seven-day week is an arbitrary and historically emergent way to divide time and that the way we use this artificial temporal structure has profound consequences for our daily lives. The week repeats itself over and over again, creating an intentionally discontinuous experience of time. Each day of the week is imbued with a distinctive character, creating a beat to the week. There are ordinary and extraordinary days, routine and non-routine, work and weekend, Mon-days and Fri-days, all because we have agreed to divide up and experience time in these ways. As fieldworkers, our observations include the consequences of both the artificial and natural temporal structures guiding our subjects' lives.

In this next exercise we are going to start capturing what we see not only by recording the activities we observe but also by noting the time when they happen. This "time-stamping" exercise will help create a temporal mapping of what you observe. It's a first, simple step in becoming aware of (1) how time is associated with the behaviors we observe in the field, and (2) how we can inject more rigor and usefulness into our observations by paying attention to the element of time.

Noting the time of something you observe provides you and anyone accessing your work with an important point of reference. Let's say that we want to compare what happened with one gorilla during one hour of observation with what happened with that same gorilla during another hour-long period on a different day. As soon as we decide we'd like to compare behaviors from two different sessions, temporal benchmarking becomes one of a fieldworker's most useful tools. For now, we're using something very simple and well understood as our benchmarks: the date and the time of day. Seconds, minutes, hours, days—these are all standards that we can use to provide a temporal spine to what we see. By noting the time of what we see, we are much better able to track, re-present, analyze, and compare our observations later.

This is such a simple and—once you think about it—obvious practice for a fieldworker. Yet few ethnographers incorporate it into their routine. You can give yourself a wonderful gift by inserting a little practical attention to time into your observation notes.

There is one other aspect to this exercise. To really stretch ourselves mentally, let's think a little more about the ways temporal structures might affect the lives of our subjects. For now, I want you to become more aware of the impact of artificial temporal structures on the behaviors you observe, particularly in light of how these things impact your own behavior.

In this exercise, then, I also ask you to think about, for instance, the relationship between your own way of carving up and experiencing time and that of the individuals or organization you are studying. If we conduct our fieldwork according to a weekly schedule, do our subjects also have a circular temporal structure that operates on top of a linear one, defined by a seven-day period? Does their cycle of time peak on the same day as ours? Is each day of our subjects' week distinct from the others? Does this reflect the same distinctions in how we experience our own week? Are any weeks (or months) in the year distinct from the others? Are these the same for our subjects as they are for us?

It is important that we understand our subjects' temporal landmarks. Do these landmarks function in the same way for them that

Zerubavel argues they do for us—preventing us from being "lost in an endless series of days—as gray as fog—confus[ing] one day with another?" (136). Does the week also protect our subjects "from the frightening truth that the sequence of days is not circular at all, but linear"? (84). These become even more interesting questions when studying a nonhuman species, particularly because we have to answer them based only on what we observe. This is a worthy challenge for any fieldworker.

If we are to truly understand our subjects' lives, we should apply ourselves to the question of how their activities are structured and scheduled across time. How does that happen across an hour, a morning, a day, a week, a month, or a year? We must structure our fieldwork accordingly to answer each of those questions. The *Seven Day Circle* gives us a starting place. Look for all the dimensions of time addressed there: artificial v. natural; circular v. linear; pulsating v. nonpulsating; ordinary v. extraordinary; routine v. nonroutine; workweek days v. weekend days; Mondays v. Fridays, and so forth.

The importance of artificial time in creating behavioral constraints applies even if one studies wild animals in a human setting. The time of day affects homeowners' comings and goings, the amount of traffic on the roads, when the man down the street feeds the pigeons, or moms bring their kids to the park. The days of the week determine garbage pick-up, lawn mowing, laundry on clotheslines. The week in the year may mean birdfeeders as an option, pools opening or closing, special holiday gifts left for the animals, hunters to contend with, and spring fever, to name a few ways in which the season may affect wild animals' activities. Humans' artificial temporal structures layer over nature's to complicate wild animals' lives in undeniable ways.

So, here is the next exercise—a nice, specific mission to help you zero in on the temporal dimension of fieldwork.

Exercise 2—Temporal Mapping I

Select a slower-moving individual. Create a temporal map of this individual's movement by noting the time at which your observations occur. Do this by selecting a body part and describing its movements. How is this body part used across time? How does it move? What does it do? When does it do it? See how this part of the body moves relative to other parts of the body. Look for the rhythms of any synchronized movements that you notice. You can pick any part—a hand or foot, lips or tongue, an elbow, wing or fin, the abdomen, head, or butt—whatever, depending on your species, of course. Keep it simple—and watch carefully.

Note any natural or artificial temporal elements that you think might be constraining, enabling, or affecting your subject's behavior.

Here's a simple report structure that you can use for the remaining exercises. Figure on five to fifteen pages for your report, excluding appended field notes. It will depend on how image-heavy it is—photos and diagrams take up a lot of space—as well as how seriously you take this opportunity to reflect.

Your name, date of report
Exercise #
Date of observation session
Duration of observation session
Location of observation session

I. Restate the exercise
II. Set the stage: Tell me what you were looking for, what factors led to your observation choices, and what was going on around you and in your chosen field site when you began.

III. Report your specific observations and any relevant details about what facilitated or impeded your ability to make those observations.
IV. Summarize any general insights you gained.
V. Reflect back on the process: What was most challenging for you? What do you think worked especially well? Any unexpected glitches or insights? Is there anything you'd do differently if you did this again? Is there anything you'd like to follow up on next time, perhaps something you'd like to know or an aspect of the process that you'd like to concentrate on?
VI. Attach scanned copies of your field notes, for easy, future reference.

I recommend that you do not read further until you have completed this exercise, including the report based on your fieldwork.

11:48 LIPS - RESTING , CLOSE TO GROUND
SLIGHTLY OPEN.
closed

Kowali is resting her head, her face is close
to the ground and her lips are slightly open.

11:46   11:48   11:50

Post-Exercise Discussion

For the most part, I break my discussions of the responses to these exercises into three parts. I focus first on the conceptual part of the challenge, second on the mechanics of the exercise, and third on writing up your report. I continue to intersperse my answers to common, important questions related to each exercise throughout these discussions.

Today's Conceptual Challenge

This exercise should help you think more intentionally about the concept of time and how to use it to enrich your research. Again, temporality is most fieldworkers' weaker hand. We must isolate, think about, and exercise it more often and in a more concentrated fashion to bring it up to speed with what tends to be our greater strength, the spatial dimension of the field.

In addition to thinking more about time, I hope you gleaned some fresh insights from thinking about the ways natural and artificial temporal structures constrained what you saw. Remember that these temporal structures can influence us in very general as well as quite specific ways. If, for instance, the sun is out and you are watching a diurnal species, then your subjects are probably up, out, and about at least in part because of natural time. As Zerubavel reminds us, though, schedules—whether daily, weekly, monthly, or yearly—are artificial. If the individuals you were watching were doing what they were doing because of a human's scheduled expectation that they do so at that time, then your subjects were influenced by artificial temporality as well as natural. We'll discuss this in more detail shortly. For now, the important point is to think about the different ways that time contributes to what you see in the field.

Why would you want to think about temporal structures? First, there is the analytical value of this kind of exercise. It's important not to contain your analysis to the micro-level of getting, translating, and communicating raw data. We should always step back from the data, looking down and over and through it to see the bigger picture of which it might be a part. This is how we find the patterns that scientists should look for, along with the sources of those patterns. Temporal structures result in behavioral patterns, which then reflect back on and sometimes modify the structures, themselves.

Second, taking note of artificial temporal structures has practical value. These social phenomena are interesting in and of themselves, as are their consequences for our behavior. However, artificial temporal structures should not be reified. They can and sometimes should be altered to better accommodate existing behaviors. If we realize that a behavior appears in response to a schedule, then we also know what we can change if we want to stop that behavior or displace it to another time.

This is exactly what Leslie Perlow (1997) found. In *Finding Time*, Perlow reports that software engineers' productivity and ways of working change radically depending on how the firm schedules parts of their days. By providing short, well-defined periods each day in which co-workers agreed not to interrupt each other, she showed how people could get far more work done and meet their deadlines with far fewer heroics.[1]

Altering a schedule could begin to solve other social problems too. We now know that if US teenagers were allowed to follow their biological clocks, they would stay up later at night and sleep later in the mornings, needing about nine hours of sleep altogether. Yet the artificial temporal location of the school day opposes the natural night-owl cycle of adolescent physiology. High school students typically start their school day first, well before primary grade children. From a design perspective, if we think it is important for teenagers to be at their best during the day, they should have the latest school start time, not the earliest.

In terms of other species, birds are highly dependent on a series of behavioral consequences related to our artificial temporal structures. Residential urban birds have taken to singing at night to advertise their presence and availability for mating, as they cannot be heard above city noise during the day. Of far greater importance to the species, though, are the hundreds of millions of migrating birds killed each year when they track onto the nighttime lights and reflective glass of urban buildings, flying directly into the windows.[2] Our desire for artificial twenty-four-hour-day city living has a devastating impact on bird populations around the world.

In response, the Campaign for Dark Skies aims to benefit both birds and humans by encouraging cities to reduce if not eliminate the artificial nighttime lights and temporality we bestow on the world. The goal is to revert cities as much as possible back to the natural, diurnal temporal order that guides avian behavior to help protect the species from the consequences of their instincts. Efforts increase especially during peak migratory times to accommodate the birds' natural daily and annual temporal patterns.

Not every fieldworker can intervene to change the problems they observe. Not every fieldworker wants to. However, many of the fieldworkers I know are designers and they are paid to do exactly that. The more any of us can identify an artificial cause of unwanted and especially unnecessary consequences, the more power we have to change these things. Time is an often hidden, but important influence on behavior.

The Mechanics of This Exercise

Keeping track of time is part of daily life for modern citizens. Many of us are acutely aware of the precise time of day—down to the minute, in fact. As fieldworkers, we should incorporate that awareness into our note-taking practices.

If sensitivity to time in the field is new for you, it can take a little while before it starts to feel automatic. Don't worry if you found yourself frantic as you shifted attention between the clock and other matters; this is normal at first. As long as you have a time-keeping device in view, you just need to become more mindful of the need to use it.

You may have become aware of other important issues while tackling this assignment. For some students, this is the first time they wonder if what they see is "normal." They wonder if they affect what they're watching, just by being there.

Any researcher should be concerned about the consequences of our presence on what we see in the field. Introductory sociology students learn about the Hawthorne Effect, named for the factory in which researchers found that simply by watching the employees, the workers' productivity increased. Sociologists are not alone in this concern. In physics, scientists hypothesize that simply making a measurement changes what is being measured.

Some ethnographers go undercover to minimize this effect. Without their co-workers' or management's knowledge, such researchers take a job in a factory or store, or join a cult, militia, police department, and so forth. Special standards must be met for this research to be approved by institutional review boards. In part, the researcher must demonstrate that the findings can only be obtained in this way and that the benefit from the research outweighs the potential costs of such deceptive work.

But is it possible to at least minimize the effect of one's presence on the field without actually going undercover? A researcher is a stranger who would never normally be there. This can make a fieldworker a highly visible entity, especially if one is new to a particular field. Fortunately, a person's visibility can change over time.

One becomes less noticeable by becoming more familiar, more expected, more taken for granted as time goes on. This is precisely how ethnographers generally overcome the worst hurdles that prevent us from learning how people normally behave and how things normally happen in our field sites—by we, ourselves, becoming normalized and our subjects becoming desensitized to our presence. Eventually, we may even benefit from our marginal status, in Robert Parks's (1928) sense of the term, where we are both insider and outsider, privy to the world we wish to understand while able to understand it in ways that full members cannot.

This same process applies to interspecies fieldwork. However, observing other species can make us even more mindful regarding our subjects' awareness of and responses to our presence. It can do this in quite unexpected ways.

Ethnographers generally delight in the moments when we suddenly realize that we are accepted in the field. We revel when granted access to information and places withheld from outsiders, a sign we have developed good relationships with our subjects. We congratulate ourselves on having said the right things to the right people, on managing the situation so well that it has resulted in this fortunate outcome.

Our *non*verbal communication does not get the same level of attention as the words we say, yet it, too, contributes greatly to our relationships in the field. Observing nonhuman, especially undomesticated animals, forefronts this element of fieldwork in a big way. With these subjects, especially, it's the nonverbal ways in which we conduct ourselves that will or won't gain our subjects' trust. Watch any film of Jane Goodall observing her chimps and you will immediately see what I mean.

The big secret about zoo animals, for instance, is that they watch us while we watch them. Go often enough, long enough, and respectfully enough, and they will almost certainly begin to single you out, recognize you, and possibly attempt to make a connection with you. You don't have to feed them. You don't have to touch them. You do, however, need to signal that you are not a threat, and, in fact, that you actually respect them. The goal is to transmit an unassuming, easy, quiet, respectful, and reassuring presence with as self-contained and minimal a footprint as possible. This is no different with human subjects and you already have years of experience in knowing how to do it.

If you are studying another species, however, it is especially important that you find out what to do—and what not to do—to create a respectful relationship with them. It turns out that field-workers studying gorillas are likely to transmit meaningful messages to their subjects quite effectively without having a clue they're doing so. Many years ago, one of my students sat down on the concrete ledge in which the glass wall separating the gorillas and the zoo visitors was embedded. The student seated herself sideways on the ledge with her right shoulder against the glass, toward the gorillas. She took out her notebook and began alternating between looking up to watch the gorilla on the far side of the habitat and looking down to make notes. She'd look up to observe, look down to scribble, over and over again.

About ten minutes into her session she finished writing and looked up again—right into the face of a gorilla toddler, about three inches away. The toddler looked deeply into her eyes, then sat down and leisurely looked the student over before finally moving away. Excited note-making followed. Just as the student looked up again, however, an adult female gorilla body-slammed the glass exactly where the student was sitting. Startled right off her makeshift bench, the student was left semi-standing, juggling her things in heart-racing astonishment.

Here's what I think happened. Polite, relaxed gorillas spend a lot of time sitting in profile relative to each other, head slightly down.

They glance quickly and reassuringly at each other out of the corners of their eyes, sometimes briefly lifting their heads when they do so to emphasize their awareness of and sociability toward their troop mates. If another gorilla looks at them, they will quickly glance away, often looking downward to indicate the same state of mind. In addition to using specific postures and eye contact, gorillas also signal respect by *not* showing their teeth. Gorillas laugh, but they do not show their teeth to indicate happiness. In general, bared teeth signal either play-fighting or aggression and fighting for real.

Infant and toddler gorillas haven't learned any of this yet, so they are excused from what would be unacceptable behavior in older gorilla kids and adults. Little ones will look openly at other individuals in curiosity or potential friendship, maintaining eye contact much longer than adults. The kids violate spatial norms and come much closer to individuals than older children and adults would. And if they're feeling brave, they will engage with any and all other creatures and objects, including human strangers.

And so there was my student, sitting in profile at the same level as the gorillas, repeatedly glancing up and looking down, with a nice, neutral face, focused on her work. She could not have done a better job signaling "I'm a super respectful gorilla who finds you all very interesting." It's no wonder the toddler noticed her and came over to check her out. And it's no wonder the mother appeared shortly thereafter, making it clear to both student and toddler that they should stay away from each other. In sum, the right nonverbal communication directed toward a gorilla can be the same as candy in the hands of human strangers—even if it's only a good, watchful mom who realizes it.

An encounter like this uniquely brings home the importance of nonverbal communication for a fieldworker. Like an ethnomethodological experiment, observation-based research on other species can bring our attention to what would be fundamentally taken for granted if we stuck only with human subjects. Our presence is also transmitting constant messages like these when we study people but we are less likely to realize and rely on it as a tool that can be used to our benefit.

Interestingly enough, by continuing to behave as a polite, respectful gorilla over the coming weeks, the student eventually succeeded in getting the mom to become more relaxed around her. To my knowledge, the toddler never came that close again. That may have been the mom's only concern all along. However, the desensitizing process that normally works to fieldworkers' advantage with human subjects seems to have worked on this initially resistant mother too.

A second hidden yet obvious aspect of this story bears highlighting: the effect of your proximity to your subjects. Visibility to your subjects is not only affected by whether or not you quietly watch in a polite fashion. Your visibility is also enhanced if you stick out from the background—whether you are in close proximity to your subjects, or visibly watching in isolation, from afar. A lone researcher sitting at the top of a stadium watching a football team practice can attract as much attention as one who plunks her stuff down on the team bench.

The position from which you choose to watch your subjects is highly significant not only because it affects their awareness of you but it also affects your field of view. Whether you are close, far, or within some middle distance, your proximity to your subjects will let you see some things quite well and others not so well. You may have noticed in this exercise that you had an excellent vantage point to see some things but not others. Did you take the opportunity to move as you wished to get the variety of data you wanted? We don't always have that option, but it is important to be aware of the ways in which your field of view may be privileging your perspective as well as handicapping it.

If you are close to the habitat glass walls watching gorillas, for instance, you can focus in on faces and body parts. That would be an excellent vantage point for this exercise—assuming your subject didn't get up, move, and then become inaccessible to you. For other exercises, it would be better to step farther back so that you could more easily capture the gorillas' comings and goings relative to each other and throughout the entire habitat. If you wanted to observe and track visitors' behavior throughout a building, you would need to pull back even farther, so you could scan the full length of the structure.

Whoever your subjects, it's a good idea to walk around your observation site each day before you commit to a location for taking data. Try to get the best view for what you're interested in. If you can, be ready to move to see what you need to see, too. As long as you don't have to stay put, it's not a bad idea to move every once in a while, just so you can see what you couldn't see before. You may decide you were already in the perfect place and go back, but there can be interesting reveals by shifting your vantage point. Don't be afraid to sit, stand, squat—whatever helps you find a new way of looking without attracting too much attention.

To sum up, having an observer present may affect what is happening in the field. The more visible you are to your subjects, the more this will be the case. Our job is to minimize our visibility and any negative effects that might result from our presence. This is one dimension of what it means to conduct ourselves in a way that allows the best chance of fulfilling our missions each time we are in the field.

There is another question that some students ask during this exercise. Roughly, "Is it okay to ask other people in my field site for information about what I'm seeing?" These students worry about missing important information that regulars (people normally found at the field site) would know. Used to putting the acquisition of correct information above other priorities, such students want to supplement their observations by questioning those who they suspect know what's going on better than they do.

The answer to this question is, of course, no, you should not ask other people for information about what you're seeing. Not yet. There are at least two reasons. First, don't take any shortcuts. Struggle to figure things out for yourself; it's worth it. Be Darwin on the *Beagle*, Mead in Samoa. If you are a true scientist, this is already part of your make-up. A motivated and properly skeptical scientist would not accept anyone else's account of an intriguing puzzle if they could observe the situation and figure it out for themselves. Doing so brings a genuine sense of joy and accomplishment. Learn how to watch closely, estimate what you cannot know precisely, describe in detail, and build your own mental model of what you see. Later, when you've rediscovered your inner scientist and know how to find the information on your own, you can take shortcuts and risk asking other people to tell you things that you're dying to know. But not now.

The second reason has to do with a much bigger question— why would we ever bother to independently observe behavior if we can just ask people about what's going on instead? The short answer is that often we can't—or shouldn't. Trusting others' accounts, alone, is frequently not in our best interests. Observation methods can give us answers—or clues to answers—any time we do not wish to rely on another individual serving as intermediary for the information we seek.

Sometimes others don't know what we want to know. We can ask, and they can have the best of intentions, but what we get is what our conversants believe or wish was happening, rather than what *is* happening. Sometimes they lie, intentionally giving us false information—possibly for understandable reasons. And sometimes people just don't have the ability to describe what they do in a way that would be as useful to us as if we watched them do it. The more well-defined your scholarly agenda, informed by all the sensitizing concepts in your analytical framework, the more this will be the case. The point is, while our subjects' insights can be incredibly valuable in informing what we think and do, we have to recognize this information for what it is—other individuals' explanations and accounts—which is not the same as the reality they describe.

The differences between what people tell us and what we observe can be a wonderful entry point for our research. Ask people why they do things, what they would like to do, and what they think they do. Then compare their answers with their actual behavior, as you've observed it. This is a great way to generate insights and identify opportunities for helpful intervention. The discrepancy between subjects' intentions, beliefs, and desires, and what is actually (or could be) happening, is a sweet spot for any fieldworker.

Conversation may nonetheless be part of your data when you are doing these exercises. If you overhear people saying something that you find relevant to your mission for the day, you may consider it data. It is something you observed. It is different from interview data where you solicit information from someone.

Imagine you are watching people in a checkout line to study whether or not a new store layout is working. You may certainly keep track of the conversation you overhear as well as the nonverbal communication you witness. This is different from going up to customers and asking "did you have to wait longer than three minutes to checkout today?" or "did you pick up an additional item for purchase today while waiting in line to check out?" It might be reasonable to ask this for such a study, although you could do the observation and get the answers yourself. It would be a far more interesting study if you had both observation and interview data about the answers to these questions. But for a strictly observation-based exercise, you can only watch and listen, not interact with your subjects. The fastest way to gain the skills necessary to do this well is to avoid relying on others for information and get it yourself.

A third question often raised during this exercise is "When should I take written notes versus sketching, photography, or other data capturing methods?" Deciding how to best note what you see is a significant challenge as well as an excellent opportunity for fulfilling our creative urge. Perhaps you tried sketching for this exercise. Perhaps you tried taking photographs. Perhaps you inter-mixed either or both of these with written or typed notes. I hope you thought about this question; it means you have an open mind about the nature of field notes.

The challenge of a mixed media approach to note-taking is threefold: (1) mastering different forms of documentation and fig-uring which to use, when, (2) mastering the mechanics of each and of switching between them, and (3) deciding how to use these dif-ferent types of data in your write-up.

First come the decisions we make about the forms of our doc-umentation. These are influenced in part by how versatile we are with each form and how each constrains the documentation process. Whether taking notes mentally, by hand, on a keyboard, with a camera, by sketching, or by audio or audio-visual recording with later transcription, each presents advantages and disadvan-tages.

"Head notes," as Emerson calls them, are wonderfully unob-trusive. They do not interfere with the observation process or the researcher's relationship with the observed in ways other tech-niques might. Yet this technique leaves us at the mercy of our mem-ories. Most of us will do better creating some record of our data, while we are creating it. Jotting notes down on paper by hand is the most familiar option along these lines, which can be fast, minimal, and highly customized.

Sketching—particularly with the addition of color—allows one to see, know, and understand the subject in a remarkable fashion. Eduardo Corte de Real (2009) is an architect and designer known for capturing and understanding the world through his line drawings. He once told me that the reason drawing is so effective in helping you to understand what you're looking at is because it requires you to "touch" every part of the subject with your eyes. It can be quite an intimate way of understanding what one observes. Photographs, on the other hand, provide unmatched speed and control over the scope of what one captures, allowing an observer to freeze activity in time and allowing extraordinarily careful analysis later.

Audio recording is unparalleled for those who wish to capture all dimensions of sound, whether for the simplest analysis of our subjects' vocal utterances or the full auditory environment we are studying, or the closest possible analysis of sound waves such as those used in the research of linguists. (For example, see primatologist Andrew Halloran's (2012) remarkable *Song of the Ape* on chimpanzee dialects.) Audio-video recording can provide the most complete capture of field data and be remarkably useful in supporting one's claims as a result. Digital photographs and audio and visual recordings have the additional ability to include time stamps for us—and even to capture data automatically for us at predetermined intervals, which can be especially welcome for exercises like this one.[3]

Each form of documentation encourages a given researcher to understand what is observed in a different way, further influencing the choice of how to document it. Some fieldworkers may come to know their subjects better by photographing them, as this method allows them to study and engage their subjects in ways that the process of creating written descriptions does not. Yet fieldworkers gifted in written expression may find that writing about what they see is the best way for them to understand it.

The ability to swiftly change and move between different methods also influences our choices in how to document what we see. It can be difficult for a novice—or someone deeply involved in one particular method—to use more than a single way of collecting data. Without the ability to seamlessly switch between them, one might be better off sticking with a single form of capture rather than risk missing things. Some individuals might find that any device is one device too many, and prefer to rely strictly on the naked eye and ear—even if one might later regret not having other representational forms of what was seen.

A third factor affecting our decisions is the issue of what is best captured and communicated by each form. Illustrations have advantages and disadvantages relative to photographs, black and white images relative to color ones, images relative to written representations, numerical summaries compared to qualitative ones, and so on. By experimenting with each of these ways of understanding and communicating one can make the most fully informed decision of what to rely on and when, given the associated trade-offs. There are volumes written on this subject and it is precisely the job of user-centered visual communication designers to make such decisions for the rest of us, given the information that is available, the target audience, and what one wishes for them to retain from the material presented.

Even if we, personally, decide not to pursue mastery of any of these techniques, it is well worth developing knowledge of the value of each. There are always collaborators and paid professionals who can lend us their skills when our own are lacking. We simply need to know enough to know when and who to call on for help.

Other considerations may further constrain your decision on when to use what type of data-capturing technique. Photography, for instance, has a special ability to capture likenesses and actions. If your subjects are humans—and especially if you've promised them anonymity—then they may get antsy seeing you photograph them. Trying to photograph children or employees doing their jobs, for example, could get you into trouble pretty quickly and you might avoid it for that reason. These days, however, anyone is likely to be worried about privacy and wary of ending up as a meme or named in someone's lawsuit. Even if you get good at covert photography techniques and lessen the attention you draw to yourself while photographing others, you will need to take special care to ensure the protection of any photographs you take.[4]

If you do fieldwork in the United States, you should know that social scientists do not necessarily enjoy the same privileges of protecting their sources as do journalists. I was a graduate student in the same program as Mario Brajuha, whose dissertation field notes on what he saw and heard in the restaurant where he had been working were subpoenaed as part of an arson investigation after the establishment burned down (Brajuha and Hallowell 1986). After a protracted legal battle, Brajuha was allowed to redact his field notes before handing them over to the judge, but the case cost him dearly emotionally and financially and established a precedent that every fieldworker should keep in mind.[5] In short, if you record something in any way, there is always a possibility—if a minute one—that the information could become public in ways you might never imagine. It is not just hackers that social scientists need to worry about.

A fourth and final cluster of questions in response to this exercise gets to the heart of the analytical fieldwork approach. The issue is articulated something like this: "I was so focused on my chosen body part that I had no idea what was going on with the rest of this individual's body. I had no idea what was going on with the rest of the group, either. If we're so focused only on what we're interested in, doesn't that mean we will miss other things?" This is a central issue for this book and it deserves a somewhat lengthy response.

First, if we pose these questions differently, like "Do we only see what we are prepared to see? Will we miss other things because we're not expecting to see them?" then with the approach I advocate, the answer is yes, inevitably. It is critical, then, that we are crystal clear about what we want to prepare ourselves for, how we will do it, and what we will do to make sure we miss as little as possible of anything related to our interests.

You will need to pick the questions you ask and the ways you answer them very carefully. Logically, for each question you decide to focus on, you will ignore many other possibilities. The same holds true if we engage in traditional, more loosely structured fieldwork; we are simply less likely to realize it in that approach.

It is far better to be fully aware that when we choose to pursue one line of inquiry, we are also choosing to not pursue others, and to pick each of your foci of attention for the day with great intentionality. Knowing that the decision to focus on "Kwan's right foot" means that we are not going to find out much about what his left hand or right ear are doing makes us think more strategically about that choice. It helps us prioritize and follow through on what we think most matters during our fieldwork. That is the advantage of this approach.

Once clear about what you are interested in, additional courses of action can better prepare you for seeing everything happening in the field that is related to your interests. These courses of action include (1) thinking broadly about your interests and the concepts, categories, and relationships of which they might be a subset; (2) taking data in a way most likely to expose you to unanticipated, unexpected behaviors and events; and (3) taking seriously each piece of data in your analysis, no matter how anomalous it may seem.

Begin by thinking broadly about what your interests really are, like a formal sociologist would. As a rule, that means focusing on concepts, on categories, on relationships (between categories as well as people), and on the most general characteristics of a behavior or situation. Lift your research interest to its highest analytical level and then think about other phenomena, situations, relationships, and behaviors associated with its most general form. Rather than a single specific body part, object, topic, relationship, type of interaction, or situation, think of your interest as a manifestation of others and use each as a mental entry point into yours. Realize that specifics serve as instances or examples in which higher-level, more transcendent concepts play out. Kwan's right foot, for instance, is related to a variety of concepts: mobility, balance, use-value, symmetry, thumb, cushioning, standing, walking, grasping, playing. Each could provide an interesting sensitizing function for your research on how he uses it.

Let's say you are interested in something more typically sociological, like interactions between female and male soldiers in today's military. The precise natures of these interactions are the focus of your research at one level, but you are probably also interested in concepts that are manifested in these interactions. Male-female soldier interactions are entry points into higher-level concepts like warrior, soldier, gender, social role, woman, man, mother, father, son, daughter, power, hierarchy, status, institutions, discrimination, prejudice, race, ethnicity, age, equality, inequality, abuse, career, job, and more. You could read and think about these concepts, then plan days in the field around them—as well as using them to write up your findings later. By pursuing data about your specific interest from this much richer perspective, it helps you look for related behaviors and incidents you might not see otherwise.

You can also focus on the highest-level description of your interest to get the broadest possible data set to think with. Let's say you're interested in a specific, applied problem, like designing a better way for families to secure the files on their computers. It is very easy to hack most residential users, largely because of the ways in which they interface with the web. You can begin and end with this design problem and the most obvious computer user interactions as your focus of attention, getting some rich data by simply watching what people do when they use their computers.

You can also sensitize your observation time by thinking about the concepts that might be manifested in the behaviors you will probably see. Technology, property, ownership, security, protection, defense, self-defense, attack, network, privacy, citizen, criminal, family, parents, masculinity, femininity, competence, surveillance, plotting, planning, service design, are just some examples. These can then drive specific sessions of fieldwork and its write-up.

You can also think of your particular interest as an example of one or more general situations. For instance, you could think of the computer user and the hacker, as "someone who has something that someone else wants." This will lead you to think of—and perhaps study—other situations that fall into this category and the concepts and behaviors associated with them.

It can be enlightening to think about any research question this way. It enlarges your perspective while helping you better identify and define the specific example in which you are interested of this larger situational category. The structural dimensions that help define what is common and unique to each related situation readily emerge from taking this approach, including the range of people, relationships, behaviors, and spatio-temporal locations associated with each specific manifestation of the larger category.

In this example, let's spend a bit of time thinking about the relationship category of "people who might want something that you have." It could be:

- A friend, asking to have or share what you have—or not even having to, because you know they'd like it
- A friendly looking stranger clearly in need

- A disheveled, disorderly, deranged stranger clearly in need
- A bartering partner (loosely defined) such as a retailer, employer, neighbor, fellow hobbyist, etc.
- A con(fidence) man
- A stealthy thief such as a little brother, adulterer, pickpocket, car thief, cat burglar, hacker, etc.
- An individual or corporate entity bringing suit against you
- The State, in any form, e.g., IRS, police, DMV
- Bullies/muggers/intruders with a range of possible behaviors, such as threatening to assault, assaulting, assaulting with a deadly weapon—doing these personally or via hired muscle

The list could go on, and the more time you devote to it, the richer the range of behaviors, concepts, scenarios, and relationships to which you will sensitize yourself. In the process, you will be making yourself better prepared to see something happening in the field. You will also have a good idea about whether or not it might be related to your specific interest, that is, how to increase computer security for residential users.

These categories of "people who might want what we have" have subcategories nested within them too. There are all kinds of friends, con men, and hackers, each with their own list of normative behaviors, scenarios, and motivations. The deeper we go then, the more it can lead us into thinking about these relationships and the behaviors, motivations, and emotions that the actors involved have experienced for millennia.

From this perspective, today's computer-using family member—no matter how good their computer defenses—may be seen as just another variation on an ages-old story in which "some people try to take things away from other people." The "wannahaves" use a variety of techniques that are more and less direct, persuasive, visible, physical, and so on. These have a variety of consequences for the well-being of the person who possesses the coveted object as well as for the individuals who would like to have it. Whatever you see happening in the field could now be viewed from this higher-level relationship-category perch as well as the situation-category perspective, or just the straightforward, micro-interactionist one. Taking any such higher-level approach means that you will be more likely to see a greater range of otherwise less intuitive data that is relevant to your research interests.

Thinking through the broadest possible range of *behaviors* that we might associate with any of these concepts, situations, or relationships, can also provide a wealth of possibilities for seeing relevant data that others might miss. It might bring to mind metaphors and analogies that could shed a powerful light on what we see in the field. These may let us recognize and make sense of behaviors—or (even better for designers) possibilities for new behaviors—from new, useful angles.

If we think about the concepts *security, defenses,* or *self-defense,* we might suddenly see our residential computer users either engaged in—or perfectly suited for—some familiar, ages-old defensive tropes. Their behaviors and technological choices might reflect a defensive position based on (1) camouflage, digitally hiding their machines, their data, and possibly even their relative lack of protection in plain sight; (2) the digital equivalent of a moated castle, with archers poised to unleash arrows, catapults with boulders at the ready, and a cauldron of boiling oil to pour on any successful breachers' heads; (3) the use of others' protective services, whether through purchase, like mercenaries, or through alliances with those who will help in times of need; or (4) institutional retribution—the equivalent of going to the monarch or priest for justice, after the fact.

It may now be clearer why my approach makes so much room for the distinct gifts each fieldworker brings to the table. When one approaches the field this way, individual fieldworkers' special knowledge—special ways of looking at the world—inevitably result in unique collections of data, unique ways of analyzing that data, and unique ways of communicating that data to others. I have met, interviewed, or witnessed people attempting to achieve computer security through each of the medieval defensive categories of action I've just described. Obviously, any fieldworker with expertise in military history, martial arts, fencing, wrestling, football, psychology, architecture, or civil engineering, to name but a few possibilities, could produce a different way of imagining and organizing the potential defensive behaviors of computer users. Any of us might possibly see data where the other does not, for that reason. But if we all think about our subject of interest as an example of as many relevant concepts, situations, relationships and interactions as possible, then we will each stand the best chance of collecting the fullest data set and producing the most correct and interesting conclusions based on it.

At the very least, thinking about your work from this kind of perspective—as a specific type of a more generalized case—can broaden your understanding of what might be relevant data when you do see it. It will help you collect a richer data set. It will help prevent you from getting cognitively locked in by low, superficial expectations, prepared to see only certain specifics and missing those that might be most revealing to you.

A second way to best prepare yourself to not miss observations related to your interests is to take data in a way most likely to expose you to unanticipated, unexpected behaviors and events while you're in the field. Plan your observation time carefully so that you focus not only on the generalized concepts, categories, situations, relationships, and behaviors that you've decided are relevant, but also so that you do this at times and in ways you might not otherwise. This entire book focuses on helping you develop this approach to your observation sessions, so stick with the exercises.

A third way to not miss relevant data is to not dismiss the relevance of any confirmed instance, case, or data point even if it appears anomalous. If you take it seriously, a data point that does not confirm what you think is going on—that does not seem to fit with the model or findings that you have, up until that point, believed were correct—can drive you to an even better, more correct conclusion. There is no smoothing the fit for an ethnographer, no data interpolation permitted. You must account for the full data set. If you know something is real and you know it is relevant, but your model does not and cannot account for it, then you must assume your model is wrong. Think of your findings so far as only a subset of the real insights waiting for you, and keep working the problem. This, too, is an essential part of preparing one's self for this kind of fieldwork.

There is one more issue related to focus in the field that you were likely to encounter during this exercise. The inability to maintain a tight focus on that in which you are supposed to be interested when other things are happening is a common, persistent challenge for any fieldworker. This skill, this challenge is at the core of every exercise in this book. The goal is to be able to decide what you want to focus on in the field and then do exactly that.

To help establish your focus early on and maintain it throughout a given session remember to focus on *how* and begin with your focal point first in isolation. How does this thing in which you are interested look? How does it move? How is it used, in and of itself? This will help you keep your focus even if there is a sudden change in activity. It will help when you broaden your focus to answer these same questions relative to other parts in a system, too (e.g., this body part in conjunction with other body parts, this device as a component in a larger collection of them, this individual as a member of a team). A strong commitment to a single point of inquiry at the start will make it easier to add new concerns to the one you've already established without letting them distract and pull you away from your original subject. This is precisely why I asked you to select only one body part here and to describe it and its movements so completely—to help firmly anchor your attention on it. If you did not allow yourself to fully dwell on that body part in the beginning of your session, you probably veered away from it later—and made this challenge harder for yourself than it needed to be.

Inconsistency in the level of detail you provide in your report can be a result of inconsistency in the focus of your attention. You should expect to find some variation in what you notice and the level of detail you are able to provide as you become more familiar with what you are observing. The broader sweeps of information that we are drawn to at first become so much context as we spend more time studying our subject. However, if you found your cognitive lens more randomly zooming in and out, it could be because you were unable to resist the distraction of what was happening around the body part—possibly because of variations in the level of activity. Don't worry. You'll get better at this, too, able to be Georgia O'Keefe one day and Cezanne the next, able to not only select but also maintain whatever level of attention to detail you wish.

Today's Write-Up

Whenever we write anything, including a report based on field notes, we face the important questions of audience and purpose. I suggest that you write your report on these exercises with two people and two purposes in mind. The first person is, of course, you, and the primary reason you are writing this report is to help you think through and organize what you've done in the field in a way that also lets you practice your analytical and communication skills.

To do that, it might be useful to keep a second reader and a second purpose in mind as well. This second—imaginary—reader should be a sympathetic individual interested in what you did and what you learned in the process. This second person could be a fellow student, a professor, an expert in some aspect of the substance of your report, or just a thoughtful friend or family member. For my students this second person is me, and my role is that of an actual rather than imaginary reader. The outcome is the same: students keep in mind the fact that I will read what they write, and it influences the way they shape their reports.

In terms of the details of your report, remember to focus on the actual data in Section 3 and, in Section 4, show how your subsequent conclusions are based on that data. Present your data first (in whatever form you choose), then write down your conclusions. Next, objectively evaluate whether or not your conclusions stem directly from your data. This process will help to focus on collecting good, solid data (not impressions, not interpretations) each time you return to the field. If you can imagine a thoughtful, friendly critic reading your work as well, then your report—and your subsequent efforts in the field—are likely to be that much better.

Your report is also about your mission for the day, the particular exercise you've tackled during a given session. It should address the scholarly focus of your session (the concepts, behaviors, and other matters that interest you); the mechanics of operationalizing your interests to gather useful data (challenges, successes, important constraints); the data itself; and any insights you've gleaned based on all of this. Whatever you choose to focus on within each area of attention is up to you, as is the way you choose to present whatever you think is important, given your intended audience.

Remember, just because you collect your data in a certain way doesn't mean you have to present it in the same way. Let's say you picked the right hand as the body part you wanted to study for this exercise. You have any number of options for how you discuss your data as you present your findings. You could do this by organizing your narrative in a straightforward way, discussing what this body part did over time, following the same chronological order in which you took your data. Your narrative could actually be little more than a chart, listing the time of each data point and what happened, with a couple sentences summarizing the overall pattern you saw.

Your narrative also could be organized around categories of activities in which this body part was involved, including descriptions of the way in which the right hand was involved and how important it seemed to be for each activity. Assuming you got this kind of information, your narrative could be organized according to how much time the body part was involved in each activity you identified, from greatest to smallest amount of time—or vice versa, for example, "picking up food and putting it in his mouth—18 mins., 20 seconds," "grabbing ropes/vines, etc., 2 mins. 5 seconds" "picking nose—22 seconds," etc.

Your narrative also could be an efficient summary of multiple ways of cutting the data, each of which could be quirkier and more interesting than the last, for example, the right hand was normally held below the waist except for putting food in the mouth; the right hand came in contact with every joint except the left hip while I was watching; the left hand was engaged in concert with the right only 54 percent of the time; of the five digits on the right hand, the thumb was used the most, followed by the second (pointer) finger, the pinky, the third finger, and then the fourth; the objects with which it came in contact most often were, in decreasing order, other parts of his body, ropes/vines, food, wood chips, wood wool (also known as excelsior, made of thinly shaved aspen fibers), a rubber tube, a blanket, Mosi (another gorilla), and water; and so on. You could then finish with a rich description of the most common—or interesting—thing you saw the right hand do during your session.

My point here is twofold. First, once you have good data, you can slice it up in all kinds of interesting ways, mining it for fascinating insights. Second, you can write this up in whatever way makes sense to you. You are not limited to producing a narrative that only and directly maps on to the sequence in which you took your data, as it was happening, in the field.

How long should your report be? Some people are lavish with words, creating clarity with a literary agility much to be admired. Yet parsimony, too, can be next to godliness. Painting an accurate wordscape can be accomplished from either direction. Thus, the answer has less to do with the number of words you generate than with how effectively you use them. Use as many words as you need to produce the response that you want from your readers.

The length of your report also depends on the other ways you communicate your points. In addition to words, are you presenting concise numerical summaries? Are you using photographs or sketches or diagrams? Given the many forms of intelligence and styles of learning and communication there are, it would hardly seem correct to have a single answer to this question.

There is not even a one best way for a given researcher to answer this question—or a related question I've heard over the years, that is, "What voice should I use in my write-up?" Try them all. Use passive, active, third person, and first; be skeptical, wonder-filled, no-nonsense, and good-humored, all in turn. Feel free to play with voice. Different journals, different audiences, different projects can place different demands on the style of writing we select. Be ready to meet them all and do your best so that the way you write up something meets both your and your readers' expectations, feeling as organic, clean, and effective as possible. In field-work, versatility is an invaluable quality.

There's no one best time to write your report, either, not even for a given researcher. Everything from practical to cognitive considerations can affect the ideal time for you to write up your field notes. It is certainly good to sit down as soon as possible and fill in any factual information—any actual data—that you didn't have time to write down while you were in the field. But our data are not equivalent to our reflections on it, and it can require more time for developing our insights and writing up our findings.

Sometimes you've begun processing what you see in the field, shortly after it happened. Sometimes it's on the ride home when you realize that something was significant. Sometimes you are so exhausted that you can't think about, much less write up, anything effectively until the next day. Often it actually helps to have some distance between your sessions in the field and when you sit down to make sense of your data. If you spend the time in-between mulling things over—or stepping away from what you saw altogether so that you can return to it with fresh eyes—then waiting a while to do your write-up can be a good idea.

As you experiment and find your optimal processing pattern, you will probably find a threshold where, once you cross it, you can no longer remember things with clarity, figure out what your notes mean, or why you were so excited about your data when you were taking it. Even the best-intentioned fieldworker sometimes won't be able to get to her write-up as soon as she should. And the less interested you are in the subject, the less sleep you've had, the more activity you pack in to the time since your field session, the shorter this timeframe may become.

If you haven't already done so, now is the time to start paying closer attention to language. The distinction between observed fact and its interpretation can be obscured by anything less than the most careful use of words. Consider the difference between "the gorilla hid from view" and "the gorilla was hidden from view." The former conveys motivation, intentionality on the part of the gorilla. The latter simply states a fact, that you couldn't see the gorilla. Start looking carefully for inadvertent claims. If you cannot proofread your own work effectively, you may wish to ask someone to help you with it, so your writing better reflects your intentions.

Looking Forward

As you progress through the remaining exercises, experiment with multiple ways of exploring, capturing, and re-presenting data. The more you do so, the more you will discover the unique advantages of each method and the best permutation of approaches for each session. Make sure you take advantage of the simple report structure I have provided, too. Asking yourself to answer a few meaningful, predetermined questions can help you make faster, better sense of what you did in each exercise—and plan for the next day's effort. The report structure itself is designed to teach.

I want to finish this discussion with a quick word about relationships in the field. If you are studying a different species for the purpose of these exercises, you may be especially surprised by this element of fieldwork. Many others have written about the challenges, dangers, and rewards of developing relationships with the people we study. There are parallels when we study other species. In fact, I would argue that interspecies relationships can be especially unexpected and, therefore, especially rewarding for any fieldworker.

In part, I think this is because we often do not understand the full nature of other species or spend the protracted time with them that would better allow us to do so. Thus, this work is filled with the potential for quite memorable moments and rich connections. The sudden realization that your interest is reciprocated and perhaps even appreciated by members of a different species can be thrilling and transformative. It can change our subjects from objects into individuals to whom we have perhaps even moral obligations. It is an important lesson, in and of itself, as well as a fact that can make it especially rewarding—and sometimes, especially hard—to go to the field each day. It is early in the process right now, but if you have decided to watch another species in the same place and the same time for each of these exercises, do not be surprised if you one day find yourself the object of their study—and thinking of and experiencing your subjects in a whole new way. I hope you do.

If you wish to see some sample responses to Exercise 2 they are available at http://global.oup.com/us/watchingclosely.

Notes

1. Unfortunately, because the organization continued to reward heroic, last-minute, crunch-time behavior when it came to raises, promotions, and the like, the otherwise sensible adoption of scheduled, interruption-free time to get rid of these behaviors did not last. Changing the artificial temporal structure of the day, alone, was not enough to affect long-term change in the organization's culture. In general, my review of similar work in the sociology of organizations as well as operant conditioning experiments with other primates shows that ultimately, it is that for which primates are most immediately and visibly rewarded that most deeply affects what they do. Changes in temporal structures are often one piece—albeit a critical one—of a larger structural picture that must be altered to affect social outcomes. If Perlow's organization had changed both the temporal and the reward structures, for instance, it probably would have been quite a different place to work before long.

2. http://www.bioone.org/doi/abs/10.1650/CONDOR-13-090.1.

3. I have no doubt that mobile digital olfactory data capture will soon be available to the wider public. Food, drink, perfume, and reproductive sciences, along with knowledge passed down through millennia in different parts of the world, tell us that the scents around us may be subtly influencing human behavior and interactions, as well as that of other species. Moreover, if anyone put their mind to it, existing sensor technology could be used to track and map the materials and textures that our subjects encounter throughout their day. The Montessori tradition in education, along with many schools of aesthetic, interior, and product design, propose that the qualities of the materials we touch matter greatly in how we experience the world around us. Data-gathering tools that focus on olfactory and tactile sensation could be of great use to fieldworkers in these areas as well as others.

4. My research assistant Matt Otten designed a wonderfully secure system to meet my specifications for the digital storage of my data—and then some. In my locked office, I have an off-line PC that is never connected to the Internet and can only be used by someone with the proper log in. The hard drive is accessed

by an additional password. Any information I upload to the hard drive is encrypted on the fly. To read a copy of those electronic files, one must have the proper key/password, too. Nothing is foolproof but if we promise anonymity, then we must do our best to ensure it, especially with any data that have people's names and/or likenesses attached to it.

5. http://jce.sagepub.com/content/14/4/454.short.

Exercise Three—
Temporal Mapping II

In this exercise we draw again from the scholarship on temporality, exploring the concept more deeply. This challenge will be slightly more complicated than the last. You will (1) pay attention to (and ponder the question of) the initiation as well as the duration of an activity; (2) consider the potential rewards of analyzing your data for higher-level temporal patterns such as sequence, pulse, repetition, and cyclicality; and (3) experiment with intervals as a way of temporally sampling the field.

In *The Seven Day Circle*, we are provided the groundwork for some distinctive lessons for fieldworkers. First, this book reminds us to watch out for our own reification of time and temporal structures in the field. Be aware of how your time, as a researcher, is socially, artificially organized and how this might affect not only the data you gather but also your process of collecting it. Second, this book reminds us to use this awareness to better grasp what is going on from the perspective of those who occupy our field. What temporal structures affect their lives? How might these influence your plan to visit the field? Third, we should use our awareness of the temporal dimension to help capture what we see happening in the field in a way that makes it possible to better re-create what we see and to compare it with what may be seen at a different time. Fourth, we should use this same awareness when deciding how to re-present what we see to others. If your conclusions vary from a Monday to a Friday, for instance, or from a workday to a weekend, the way you present your conclusions should reflect that.

In *Hidden Rhythms*, sociologist Eviatar Zerubavel continues to explore the social nature of temporality, regularity, and its consequences for society. In his discussion of the organization of social life, he identifies a number of structural temporal dimensions including:

- sequential temporal structures and their often rigid manifestations;
- the uniform rates of recurrence that define so much of social life, including the cyclicality of many activities associated with the day, week, and year;
- the "pulse" or beat of a temporal sequence, around which a social unit of time builds up, peaks, and relaxes again;
- the fixed duration of many social events, that is, how long an event is expected to last; and
- the often standard temporal location of an event, that is, the "normal" time at which certain things happen.

Thus, the six critical features of an activity's or event's temporal structure are its: (1) *timing*, or temporal location, (2) *duration*, (3) *scheduled v. spontaneous* nature, (4) place in a *sequence* of events, (5) *frequency*, or rate of recurrence, and (6) potentially *cyclical* nature. By adding these temporal dimensions to our conceptual framework, we can greatly enhance our data and the quality of the insights we draw from it.

In this next exercise, we will add to our previous focus on the start of an event, by focusing on its conclusion as well. Adding duration to our description of an activity in the field completes its temporal location. It also allows us to discern other temporal elements.

Fieldworkers generally do not pay nearly as much attention to time as we do to space. One common practice illustrates this imbalance. When given free rein, researchers typically note both the starting and stopping *place* of an activity. We write things like this:

"Kwan slowly moved from the southwest corner by the window to the northeast corner by the shift door. He paused and turned to look outside twice along the way."

The time of an event is often absent. In the rare instance that we do get the time an activity started, it is almost unheard of to learn the time it stopped. Instead, our notes look like this:

"10:42 Kwan slowly moved from the southwest corner by the window to the northeast corner by the shift door. He paused and turned to look outside twice along the way."

Despite reporting both spatial bookends, we may get only one, if any, of the temporal ones.

Imagine the greater possibilities for analysis if we add the element of duration to our notes by including both the temporal beginning and ending of an activity:

"10:42 Kwan slowly moved from the southwest corner by the window to the northeast corner by the shift door. He paused and turned to look outside twice along the way. He arrived at the shift door by 10:43."

Even better:

"10:42 Kwan slowly moved from the southwest corner by the window to the northeast corner by the shift door. It took him 42 seconds to do so. He paused and turned to look outside twice along the way, for 4 seconds and 2 seconds, respectively."

Adding the duration of activities to your field notes allows for much more thorough understanding and re-presentation of what's going on in your field site.

By including duration, for instance, the last two variations immediately enrich our sense of what happened.[1] Each write-up is true and consistent with the other. But the second offers even finer granularity in terms of Kwan's nested set of activities. It almost compels us to start thinking more deeply about why Kwan moved from one point to the other in the way that he did, planting a seed of curiosity about why he turned twice to look outside. We understand not just that Kwan moved from one place to the other, but that he might have been distracted by what was going on outside—double-checking what was out there as he made his way toward his destination.

Note that if we knew the spatial distance between Kwan's starting and ending points, we could even have a good sense of his pace. Time plus distance tells us whether he was running, walking purposefully, or merely ambling over there—whether or not we also described his movement with words. With solid temporal and spatial data, we can go a long way to reconstruct events.

Detailed data like this lets you combine it in unexpected ways to answer unexpected questions later on. Collecting the duration of activities with finer detail allows for any number of unanticipated comparisons from instance to instance, session to session. This happens for two reasons. First, when you have these data, you *can* make comparisons, and you can do so with great assurance. You can quickly flip through the pages and look up the details in the heat of the moment—or much later, from the comfort of your desk. If I have excellent space and time data on Kwan's movements across the habitat, for instance, I can decide months later that I want to know more about Kwan's overall mobility throughout the day—and I can go back and calculate the percentage of his time spent, say, moving at relatively high speed, low speed, or at rest.

Second, the more you pay attention to something, the more you start recognizing and capturing patterns of behavior. You have set yourself up to recognize patterns, whether because the duration of something you just saw was so similar to or remarkably different from what you saw before. Connections and insights that you wouldn't have made otherwise can follow, and your notes may start to look more like this:

"10:42 Kwan slowly moved from the southwest corner by the window to the northeast corner by the shift door. It took him 42 seconds to do so. He paused and turned to look outside twice along the way, for 4 seconds and 2 seconds, respectively. [Note: Last week when he charged Rollie, he covered that same distance in less than 3 seconds!!]"

Duration thus provides a good example of a prime benefit of analytical fieldwork—by sensitizing ourselves and committing to this concept, we set ourselves up in the best way for seeing and capturing things that could be related to our interests.

Sometimes, getting the duration of an activity may mean you need to approximate time by counting "Mississippis," "alligators," "one-thousands" (e.g., "one, Mississippi; two, Mississippi; three, Mississippi" equals about three seconds)—or whatever method you prefer. It can be difficult to shift attention between the event you're watching and a timing device. I find it difficult even when I am braced for it, because I am glued to the action and don't want to look at the time and then write it down.

Instead, when I see something starting, I start counting off the time in my head. My sense of time is good, so I find this reliable if it's a short activity that I'm tracking. If your sense of time is not reliable, you can work on this skill. Of course, if you have a stopwatch in your hand and are well practiced with it, you can be much more precise in the data you gather. For longer, more predictable actions or events, I use a timekeeping device.

I generally know when I have either approximated time or used a watch by the nature of the action and what I've written about it. I don't have to indicate that in my notes as I've been doing this for a long time and have my personal conventions. However, if I deviate from my default convention, I make sure to indicate whether the time I've noted is approximate or precise. Once you develop your own conventions, it's only when you engage in an *unconventional* way of doing something that you should be sure to make note of it for yourself.

If you have a hard time in this next exercise noting both the precise time that an activity starts and how long it lasts, focus only on duration for a bit. Don't worry about the exact time that something starts. (Think of it as using a stopwatch rather than a wristwatch.) You can also do Exercise 2 again with this goal in mind, if you are need of practice.

Alpha? Omega?

It is not always easy to decide the duration of something. But if the goal of fieldwork is to generate new insights, thinking through duration can be hugely helpful—regardless of the species we're watching. I'll give you a small example.

No one quickly forgets the first all-out gorilla fight they witness. It is a flurry of teeth and limbs along with sometimes unbelievably fast chases and horrifying screams—truly frightening expressions of pure physical power. The first fight I saw was between Kwan (a nine-year-old male at the time, a gorilla teenager) and Helen (then the grand dame of Lincoln Park Zoo). The fight might have lasted seven interminable seconds.

Or did it? Many years later, I am now pretty good at seeing a gorilla fight in the making. I'm much better at knowing what upsets and angers individual gorillas, and what they look like when they're getting increasingly annoyed with someone. I'm also much better at noticing how long it takes an individual gorilla (participant or bystander) to emotionally recover from such an encounter, and how long it takes for the entire troop to settle back into normalcy.

I now find myself revisiting that first fight and asking the interesting questions of when does a gorilla fight really start? When is it really over? The physically violent part is the most obvious. It's the easiest to document in terms of duration. But depending on how you define a fight, identifying the initiation and conclusion to an episode of conflict may not be so easy. It depends on whether you look at the conflict as only the part that is manifested in physical contact or if you take a broader view in which conflict is sometimes signaled much earlier, through a continuum of increasingly serious and active signs of displeasure. Even the physically violent part of the conflict may not be over when you think it is.

At first, I thought that the fight I witnessed between Kwan and Helen ended in a draw. The slapping, body slamming, pushing, and teeth-baring ended as instantly as it had started. When they stopped, both combatants looked frozen in time. Their faces were about eight inches apart, eyes locked. Helen's forearm was blocking her face—and was in Kwan's mouth, his nearly two-inch canines not quite making contact from above and below. Then Kwan slowly opened his mouth even wider and retracted his neck a couple inches to carefully release Helen's arm. He backed his body up a bit and looked to his right, away from Helen. Helen stared at him the entire time. She then turned her head slightly to the right, too, looking away from Kwan in the opposite direction, but without moving the rest of her body.

At this point, I started to turn away. But Helen wasn't done. Like lightning, she turned back toward Kwan, slapping the left side of his face with her right hand, before quickly running away a few feet.

They both stood stock-still again and repeatedly glanced at each other. Then Kwan turned his back on Helen and began ostentatiously foraging for food. Helen turned her back on him and did the same. She seemed to have had the last word—at least, in that particular altercation. They moved away from each other in opposite directions, sending occasional glances backward every couple of seconds.

The rest of the adult females in the troop stayed quite still as Kwan and Helen moved away from each other. Positioned against the back wall, they kept glancing at both combatants, a bit like watching a tennis match, but moving only their eyes. The youngest nervously shifted from foot to foot, as if not quite sure what to do with herself. Within a minute, though, Kwan and Helen were as far away as they could be from each other, intent on foraging, and the rest of the troop started to emulate them.

Today, if someone asked me, "How long did that fight last?" I would not be able to give an accurate answer. When, exactly, did the friction start that led to the fight? When, exactly, did it fully dissipate?

It seems that with gorillas, as with humans, episodes of violent physical contact are exactly that—episodes in a much bigger story, a much longer string of activities and events. Bigger fights may lie dormant; they are not over. Even if one watches carefully and long enough to define the beginning and the ending of a particular episode, it is important to remember the bigger narrative of a much longer duration that could be behind what one sees at any given moment. We can do our best, but duration can be an elusive measurement.

As fieldworkers, we are always taking snapshots of a continuous stream of behavior. Our business is about identifying and collecting what Goffman called in *Frame Analysis*, "strips of activity." Accordingly, we need to get as good as we can at defining, identifying, and capturing as many nested micro-interactions as we can so that even if we can't correctly identify the start and stop of the larger narrative, we still have the best chance of describing the smaller episodes of interaction embedded within it.

If there are times when the duration of something cannot be taken for granted, there are probably more times when it *should* not be so. We want to use the field to think deeply, challenge our assumptions, and find patterns and insights others may have missed. For this reason, we should not only try to measure duration, we must also question it.

I once gave a presentation along this line to a corporate research group. It was about seeing the daily activity of shaving from a sociological perspective. I started by arguing that shaving is uniquely linked to specific conceptualizations of masculinity and femininity, adulthood and competency, status and influence, and the signaling of specific, recognizable social types and relationships. I also argued that it could be useful to think about shaving as part of a bigger, daily routine (or sequence of events associated with a special occasion) rather than an isolated act done in front of a bathroom mirror or in the shower. I showed film clips of people shaving—or pretending to do so—all part of a much bigger sequence of activities that sometimes started the day before the shaving took place.

By the time we finished, we were debating questions like "what does the act of shaving symbolize?" "How does the social, emotional, and physical environment in which the shaving occurs alter the experience?" More interestingly, we asked, "when does the act of shaving actually begin and end?" and "what do we gain by thinking of shaving as a nested activity?" Challenging the taken-for-granted aspects of what we observe—like its duration—can lead to richer insights than we might glean otherwise.

By no means do you always have to take data on duration. As with every other possibility for data discussed in this book, there may be times when you cannot collect these data due to constraints on the duration of your project, your field of view, your ability to record what's going on, and other factors. There may be times when you are not interested in duration, and it would be a waste of time to collect these data. You, your advisor, IRB, or client might decide that even though you could collect duration data, it could get you or your subjects into trouble and for that reason, you won't. We must all do our best to make an informed decision about the data we will or won't collect in any specific situation, then be prepared to live with the consequences of that decision. Data on duration are no exception to this important rule. My hope is that from now on, if you do not collect these data, it will no longer be an act of omission but a carefully reasoned choice.

Let's turn our attention to how a fieldworker might implement and use all this insight on temporality. Using the artificial system of timekeeping we have imposed on the world around us, one can note the temporal location of something and then compare that to what subjects are doing at other times. The data let us analyze subjects' behavior for patterns that seem to be correlated with time, using the results to form and answer more questions about what, exactly, is going on.

We can ask ourselves, for instance, whether the time of day, day of the week, or day of the year correlates with the behaviors we see. To answer this, we would need to find out if these activities replicate over a fixed period. We would need to start by repeating the original observation at the same time of day, same day of the week, and same duration of time for multiple weeks and comparing the results. This is a variation on what is called a time series study.

To find out if the patterns we found were representative of the entire universe of activity in our field site, however, we would have to observe the field across the entire period in question. We would collect data 24 hours a day, 7 days a week, for 365 days, and across multiple years. This would allow us to tease out the precise daily, weekly, or yearly nature of any of the behaviors we observe. Because this is so impractical, we must think carefully about what we need to know and plan our observation sessions accordingly. We should decide how to sample the field, in other words, by sampling it across time.

We might do this by trying to make sure some of our sessions are during the mornings, some in the afternoons, some in the evening, and some at night. We might rotate through days of the week and weeks of the year, sampling the activities of the field by observing at these different times. Or we might consciously sample the field during a single observation session.

The logic driving temporal sampling at any level is as follows. Although time and what happens in the field are continuous, as fieldworkers, our system of capturing what happens in the field must be discontinuous. We can never get the complete, continuous reproduction of the entirety of what is happening around us. It's just not possible to watch continuously, without a break, much less take excellent notes simultaneously.

With a well-informed and focused scholarly agenda for the day, however, we don't have to try to watch and note everything, constantly. We can—we must—be selective. We can choose precisely when we will make an observation, for how long we make it, for how long we will document it, and how frequently we repeat the process. We may make these decisions with different degrees of intentionality—from being completely unreflective and unaware of when and for how long we watch or take notes to being extremely systematic and precise about it—but make them we do.

When left to their own devices, two factors seem to drive the data-taking of most beginning students. The first factor is the perception of a change in the activity of the individual or group they are observing. The second is the students' ability to capture (that is, to note—in whatever form) what they see. Both elements contribute to the fact mentioned earlier that novice students' notes tend to document a great deal about the initiation of activities but relatively little about the middle and end. This holds true for a single activity as well as for an entire sequence. We get lots of starts but far fewer finishes.

Students' notes also tend to reflect their lack of attention to times in the field when things are relatively quiet, when they don't notice a lot of movement. Their notes reflect the perception that these are "empty" times, when one needn't pay too much attention or take what's going on too seriously. One can "take a break" because nothing interesting or notable (enough) is happening.

At the zoo, one can see a related attitude in the behavior of many visitors. The less activity among the animals, the less time visitors stay and watch. The most entitled bang on the glass and yell at animals that are quietly resting, eating, and thinking, trying to "make them do something." "Something" is, of course, an activity obvious and interesting enough for the visitors to notice it and to deem it significant.

In fact, the ways in which animals rest—much less the far larger range of more subtle activities they might be engaged in—can be hugely revealing of the social dynamics of their group, an individual's personality, proclivities, and health, and the biomechanics and daily and seasonal activity patterns of the species. An observer could use the time when animals appear to do "nothing" to reflect and learn a great deal. These are welcome opportunities for unexpected insights.

It is precisely these less active times when a good fieldworker should continue to take regular data, following up to make sure we get the middles and ends of whatever we saw initiated, and reflecting deeply on and during the relative calm to see if there is any way it might inform our scholarly interests. Just because we don't happen to notice something new happening, does not mean it's time to stop watching. Conversation analysts, for example, pay as close attention to the silences in a conversation as they do to the parts filled with spoken utterance, as these quieter moments, too, are imbued with meaning.

As fieldworkers, we must always wait, trust the plan that brought us to this site on this day and at this time, and remain determined to mine even a seemingly (but never truly) empty field for whatever insights it might contain. We must commit to seeing both the relatively positive space of our time in the field—that which is filled with activity—and the relatively negative space—which seems not to be as equally important to the overall picture. The full, complementary range of busy-ness is worthy of our attention.[2]

During the times when we perceive a lot happening, we may become keenly aware of our ability to capture what's going on. This is the second factor that drives most people's data-taking choices. When activity levels are high, it gets hard to keep track of everything. Trying to take too much data can dilute everything you do—making it all less than useful because you wind up keeping track of only what is easiest to note quickly.

Some people try not to take any notes when things are really happening. Only after things settle down do they start to recall what happened and make their notes. Sometimes this may be the best choice. But, as anyone who has transcribed an interview can tell you, the ability to recall and record a precise sequence of information can be extremely difficult, even if one tries to do so immediately after hearing or seeing it. Only those with exceptional visual memory skills can rely on this lengthy watch-and-write-later solution. One can get better at this, but the sooner one jots down exactly what one thinks happened, the better your chances are that it will be accurate.

For practical reasons, then, fieldworkers must sample what happens in the field across time. Just like quantitative social scientists who must make decisions about how to sample the universe of possibilities for their data, qualitative social scientists must do the same. The question is, will we do this with more, or less, intentionality? Will we sample only by what we happen to notice or how fast we can write? Or will we sample the field in a more predictable way, using time to direct our attention, in a way that consciously accommodates our note-taking?

To illustrate, let's imagine what the differences might be between the following two approaches to an hour-long observation session. In the first, you do your best to take continuous notes about the time and nature of the activities you see and the individuals involved. You watch what's going on and when something relevant to your interests catches your eye, you make notes, including the time it happened and who was involved. You capture not only the beginning but also the conclusion to the events you find interesting, creating a nice, organic, and complete account of the things that grabbed your attention.

In the second approach you adopt a variation on time interval research. You make an observation every five minutes during the one-hour session, perhaps deciding to note the same items at each data-collecting point that you would focus on in the first approach: the time, the nature of any relevant activity you see, and the individuals involved. You build into this every-five-minutes interval enough time so that you can carefully observe for a short period, then write about what you saw, finishing both activities before it's time to take more data.

In a perfect world—not unlike that of theoretical physics—the first data set would incorporate the second. You could extract the second and look only at that subset if you wanted. But the fieldworker's world is that of the experimental physicist, not a theoretical one. There is no perfect data set; the real world limits our measurements and analysis.

So, how representative would the first set of notes be of what happened over the duration of the hour? The attempt to start and go straight for an hour would likely leave us with some parts of the hour more documented than others, a few activities or events well represented and others missed entirely. In fact, the hour has been sampled, but perhaps not consciously—certainly not systematically.

If we followed the second approach, however, we would have twelve evenly distributed data points that might give us a better sense of what happened across the entire hour. It might miss things that the first approach might include, of course, if those things happened in-between our established intervals for making observations. But in addition to systematic sampling, the second approach has the advantage of keeping us focused but not overwhelmed. We control the data-taking process, rather than feeling as if it is controlling us.

There are distinct benefits to both ways of sampling the field. Depending on your goals, a hybrid approach might be best. That is, you will probably get the best results from your observation work by taking data at regular, predefined moments for a regular, predefined period of time, while also noting what happens in-between those predetermined moments whenever possible—particularly if it looks like it might be the start or stop of something that seems relevant to your interests.

Fieldworkers should be familiar with both approaches to taking data, so we can use each to our advantage. However, to my knowledge, few ethnographers conduct interval research in the field. Accordingly, this next exercise is designed to introduce you to this useful technique.

Both approaches to sampling the field—whatever strikes our fancy, whenever it does so versus a time-driven, interval approach—require us to make choices about when we start and when we stop observing. You can't only decide how often to take data; for each data-taking episode you must also decide for how long you will watch and how much time you will give yourself to make notes about what you saw, afterwards. You must then be ready to once again look up and begin observing again at the interval's end.

Some people using the interval approach choose a simple question and need only a glance at each data-taking moment to see what they want to know. They then record what they observed. If they have a template and it's extremely quick to fill in the data, they might decide to take data for two seconds every thirty seconds and find it a manageable task.

Others might ask a more complicated question for the day. Their data-taking interval might be every five minutes. They may decide to watch carefully for fifteen seconds, and then spend the remainder of the interval writing what they saw. If they find this unsatisfactory for some reason, they might decide to watch for one or two minutes before recording what they saw, and find they need a good five–six minutes to write that up afterward. They might have to adjust their data-taking interval to ten minutes, accordingly.

Be ready to adjust your data-gathering plan as you go. You may find you have reserved too much time for note-taking and you're twiddling your thumbs between data points. You may find you're watching for too long a period, unable to complete your notes before it's time for the next data-collection point. Or, you may find that you're missing too much and your planned observation points are unnecessarily far apart. (As time goes on, for instance, you may get faster at note-taking, or learn to make fast sketches or take instructional photographs instead of having to write out things with words. Or maybe you'll come up with an excellent form or template for recording the data you want. Any of these could lead you to increase the frequency of your data-gathering moments.) Stay tuned to the possibility of needing or wanting to adjust your sampling plans over time.

We use this same sampling logic to plan our observation sessions for an entire research project. This is not just an issue for a given session. We cannot usefully record and analyze what is going on in the field every hour of every day. We must sample the field across the coming weeks, months, or years too. Given the temporal rhythms of our field site, then, we need to plan the totality of our time there carefully, then change that sampling plan as needed, going to the field more frequently, for longer durations, or at less convenient times.

Bias is inevitable for fieldworkers. What we want to do is try to make sure our sessions are biased in ways that we think will be most useful to us. Our goal is to minimize the risk that what we observe will not tell us much about what we are truly interested in—that it will be *unintentionally* biased.

For Exercise 3, you will select an interval of time for watching and taking notes, to be repeated regularly throughout your hour in the field. Remember, to get the clearest picture of what is going on, we need data that are as temporally sensitive as possible. Start *and* stop times allow us to reconstruct not only the time at which something occurred but also its duration, its place in a sequence of events, its rate of recurrence, and any cyclicality of events relative to each other. This is what we are working toward.

At first, this may be too difficult to achieve, as the start and stop time of an interesting event may not both fall within the duration of your interval. In fact, something that you would otherwise find noteworthy may begin and end *in-between* your observation points. That can be a major drawback to interval research, if one adheres to it too rigidly.

Nonetheless, the point of this exercise is to think of the regularly occurring observation points as your main data-gathering focus. "Irregular" observation material—including what appears to be the natural conclusion to something you noticed earlier, or the start of something else that seems significant—should be seen as bonus or additional data. Initially, anything that appears between the cracks should be thought of as supplemental. Try to get the duration of activities if you want, but do not sacrifice the regular data points for the irregular ones—not at first.

Once you master the interval approach and your conceptual agenda is more clearly established, you should of course feel free to decide to follow an irregular data occurrence and abandon the regular observation points for a while. Something happening in-between your established intervals may be much more relevant to you and you should feel free to treat the temporally regular data points as more of the "get it if you can" data. For now, however, allow the lessons of the exercise to stick by staying focused on a regular rhythm of data-taking, supplementing it as you can.

Today's Exercise

For this exercise, you will need a watch with a second hand. Ideally, you might use a programmable time device—possibly a phone app—that can signal you at regular intervals. Set it to go off when you should start observing and when you should stop. If you are observing in a noisy or crowded place, headphones might make it easier to hear the auditory signals as well as block out distractions.

Temporal Mapping II: Pick an individual. Create a temporal map of this individual's activities taking data at regular, predefined moments for regular, predefined durations of time. Just for today, do not sacrifice collecting data at these regular moments for anything that happens in-between them. In your analysis of your data later on, pay attention to the duration as well as the timing, sequence, recurrence, and cyclicality of this individual's activities. Do not forget this last part of the exercise!

Be sure to look for any temporal patterns or insights your data may contain.

Set your interval to be whatever you want, but separate your observation and writing/documentation activities, alternating between them. Observe for X amount of time, write for Y, repeat. Keep adjusting the amount of time you observe, the amount of time you tend to your notes, and the overall duration of the interval until you find a comfortable pace.

If you start to flounder, try this: watch for five seconds. See how long it organically takes you to document what you saw. Set your interval accordingly. If it takes you three seconds to document your observations, you could take data every fifteen seconds, no problem. If it takes you three to four minutes to document your data, set your interval at five minutes. It's better to start with a too-short period of observation and increase it, in order to minimize frustration. You may want to try changing the ratio of observation to writing time at least three times during the exercise, in order to feel the difference. Ultimately, you want to find a good balance between watching and writing, and feel as if you are make good use of your time, overall.

(If you find it is too difficult to track multiple activities, select a single activity and track the individual's behavior with regard to just that.)

I recommend that you do not read further until you have completed this exercise, including the report based on your fieldwork.

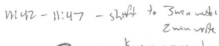

11:42 - 11:47 — shift to 3min notes
2min note

. Kwan moves to beside
tree and sits looks
outside for a long period
of time → several moments

→ he sits back w/ side
against tree and looks
around space

11:42 - 11:47

Kwan moves to beside tree and sits looking outside for several minutes.

Kwan sits back on haunches with left side against tree trunk and looks around space.

He returns to stump and leans against it.

He is spending much less time looking over towards Amare who is now with Kowali on the ground in the corner. Kwan is now primarily looking outside.

Post-Exercise Discussion

Today's Concept

If this was your first attempt at capturing the timing and duration of your subjects' activities while also looking for overarching temporal patterns, you probably found yourself struggling. Give yourself a few more tries at this exercise until you feel really comfortable with it. Hopefully, the present attempt let you see the analytical value of this kind of data despite the challenges of getting it.

Temporality can lead us to unexpected insights. For instance, *Timetables*, the 1963 classic on human behavior by sociologist Julius Roth, is a provocative study of tuberculosis patients whose recovery was unpredictable. These patients were unable to use the length of their stays in the hospital as an indicator of when they might be released. Instead, Roth found that they used "temporal benchmarks" to track their progress.

Temporal benchmarks are events recognized by a social group as indicators of significant progress toward a particular outcome. Unlike spatial milestones, Roth argues, temporal benchmarks need not be equidistant from each other, nor do they have to be the same distance apart for each individual. Such benchmarks could be signified by moving to a different part of the hospital or being allowed to participate in certain activities or receive a certain treatment. They are socially agreed-upon, meaningful, and sequential signs of progress. They allowed patients to track their recovery despite the nonconformity of the recovery process.

Temporal benchmarks can be important for fieldworkers. To find them, though, we have to pay attention to the temporal dimension. They may be spread across a self-contained event like a church service or work shift or across a longer time frame, like children's developmental histories or adults' professional careers.

There are predetermined, time-stamped benchmarks that can be relevant for specific study populations, projects, and field sites. Fiscal quarters, Black Fridays, and Cyber Mondays, for instance, help participants mark progression through the year and allow multiyear comparisons of data. Find out what benchmarks are significant to your field, by structuring the search for them and other temporal features into your fieldwork.

On the Mechanics of This Exercise

How close did you come to acquiring systematically gathered and systematically reported data? *This* is the kind of work we're aiming for—work that allows for solid analysis and well-grounded insights and interpretations. It's at the heart of science.

Did you have trouble maintaining a regular data-taking rhythm? This can be a problem if you rely on watching a clock to start and stop your observation and writing activities. If you have a smartphone or tablet, finding an app that signals the start and stop of your observation period may help. You may also want it to signal when your write-up time is about to end, so you're ready to take your next data point. If you can also independently manage a stopwatch function to track the duration of activities, that's great, but don't forget, there's always counting Mississippis.

If you kept running out of time and were unable to finish writing up what you saw, then you might need to do one of three things. First, you can reduce the duration of the observation period. If you were watching for thirty seconds before writing up what you saw, try only fifteen seconds. Increase your observation time again when you're ready.

Second, you might try reducing the number of data points by increasing the amount of time between each. If you're taking data every three minutes, try every five—or go all the way up to ten if you like. Again, reduce the duration of the interval when you're ready.

A third possibility is to refocus and redefine what you're looking for so that the data are simpler and more straightforward to collect. Ambitious daily missions typically mean collecting fewer data points with more time to document what you saw in-between them. For the purposes of learning to do interval research, make it easier to get the data you're after—for now. Trim your mission down to "what was this individual doing for the five seconds while I was watching them?" or even "did this individual have something in her right hand during these two seconds? What was it?" You can always add duration data (e.g., tracking how long the individual touched or held the thing) if you have extra time, which you probably will. Even a simple study like this could provide an interesting window into an individual's day. If it lets you comfortably explore how to do interval research, it serves an excellent pedagogical purpose too. The goal is to watch and document intently without time anxiety, whatever it takes to do that.

If you found measuring duration too challenging during this exercise, you might want to dedicate an observation session to do that and nothing else. Focus on measuring duration only; pay no attention to the nature of the activity per se, only on when it begins and ends. Make a chart and if you feel compelled to demarcate activities, just give each activity some kind of place-holder:

Activity	Duration (in minutes and seconds)
A	3 secs
B	1 min 10 secs
C	7 secs

Instead of only using letters, you could also call each activity something quick like "nose picking," "looking at me," "sitting," "eating," whatever. This might give you a chance to add up your durations into interesting categories later on, or to reflect on the sheer diversity—or monotony—of the activities you see.

When teaching a new technique, choreographers, piano teachers, and athletic coaches typically ask students to focus on mastering the requirements of one body part at a time. Once they've mastered what each part needs to do, separately, students will be better able to put it all together. Fieldworkers can learn new methods this way as well. If you can't manage taking data at regular intervals plus keeping track of the duration of specific activities, break it down. Get better at each, separately, and then try putting it all together again.

You may have been concerned about the opposite problem, however, feeling that not much was going on. You might have worried that you made a bad choice about what to observe because it wasn't challenging and you didn't get data about anything you thought was interesting. If you find the level of activity in your chosen field is too low to do an exercise effectively, consider first changing the time of your observation. The result can be as simple as the difference between watching a group of elementary school kids between 2:00 p.m. and 2:30 p.m. when they're still quietly working at desks versus watching them from 2:45 p.m. to 3:15 p.m., just before and during dismissal. Imagine also watching that same classroom on Friday at 2:45 p.m. versus Saturday at 2:45 p.m. You may need to get more information about the rhythms of your field site to find out when your study population is more active. If that doesn't work, then feel free to change who and what you're studying. When you're learning, you want a good match between what you're trying to do—the mission at hand—and the place and time in which you try to carry it out.

Find what works best for you in all aspects of observation work. Consider a fieldworker who has a challenge related to the mechanics of handwriting. Someone with dysgraphia, for example (for whom the specific combination of muscles and movements needed to write by hand with a pen or pencil is extremely challenging)— will need to find an effective alternative to how others might document their work.

Fortunately, portable keyboards of all shapes, sizes, and topographical profiles are now available. Such an individual might simply type notes in the field, or rely on a recording device to dictate them. The speech-to-text capabilities of smartphones are getting so remarkable that soon all fieldworkers might consider using them to take notes. Even left-handed fieldworkers who have no problem writing at a desk might find the task a bit trickier in the field, and may have to pay more attention to developing a system of tools and postures that works well for them.

Dyslexia may be a better-known learning disability than dysgraphia, but it is much less relevant in the field. Appearing in moderate to severe forms, dyslexia is characterized by a variety of challenges, including difficulty in decoding written language. Even after years of intervention and good progress in reading ability, dyslexia can still mean that correct spelling is a lost cause for the brightest of students.

However, because field notes are not designed to be read by anyone except the fieldworker, here's one playing field that is fairly level for a dyslexic. As long as she or he can figure out what she or he wrote down, spelling doesn't matter. The individual can spell-check while doing the write-up, perhaps using a speech-to-text application. In fact, for fieldworkers, the advantages often associated with dyslexia—superior creativity, spatial relations, and mental modeling of complex systems—far, far outweigh the disadvantages.

Dysgraphics also may have some distinct advantages in the field, of course. After a lifetime of compensating for the difficult task of writing by hand, a dysgraphic often develops a superior compensatory skillset in listening, watching, and committing to memory what she or he has seen and heard. A dysgraphic may also have gotten very good at letting a few cryptic words on a sheet of paper stand for the pages of notes that the rest of us must write in order to recall the same thing.

Such a skill is not such an asset, though, when it comes to sharing what's in your head with others—much less convincing them that your conclusions are correct. Unless dysgraphics force themselves to find a comfortable way of recording observations to share with others, they might seriously disadvantage themselves as persuasive analysts. If you're in this category, find what works for you—camera shots, DragonSpeak, audio recordings, portable keyboards—and stick with it.

Perhaps after this exercise you suspect that you suffer from an opposite problem, writing too many words in the field. Some students—often with degrees and career experience in some form of writing—are concerned that their notebooks overflow with words. If you are one of them, start by taking a look at the content of all those words. Usually, they consist mostly—if not entirely—of reflections on what the student is seeing. You may solve the problem by simply reminding yourself to focus on collecting data rather than memorializing your reactions to it. Focus on measurement rather than reaction, on numbers rather than words. Dedicate your pages to the times, durations, frequencies, distances, sizes, and locations of things. Try to do these exercises with as few words as possible and when you do use words, make sure they describe what you see rather than what you think about it.

Pay close attention to any dissatisfaction you feel with your field notes but also notice what you think works well. Do not let that go as time goes on. Success begets success in learning how to collect good, well-documented data. The analysis and eventual presentation of your insights depend on it.

Another problem for some students is maintaining a consistent unit of analysis throughout this exercise. Some have difficulty not only maintaining their focus on the individual they initially chose to study but also staying focused on an individual rather than a pair or larger group. If you are watching a social species, you may find yourself shifting from mapping what an individual does to mapping the activities of another individual too, even starting to focus on the nature of their relationship.

You may have been pulled away from your original focus in just this way; it's quite common. It is important to maintain focus, however. We can include our subject's reactions to another individual, for instance, but we must keep our attention squarely on our subject, our initial object of interest. Don't be diverted toward capturing the fullness of what this second individual is doing or start musing about their relationship. For now, only pay attention to those things that seem to be directly affecting your intended subject. If you started out intending to study multiple individuals and the relationships among them, this would be fine. But that is a different project—and different unit of analysis—than the one intended in this exercise.

Good data mean trying not to slip between foci of attention—including different units of analysis—while you're trying to collect it. It means sticking with the same mission with laser-like focus from start to finish. Switching between points of interest during a session will not develop your ability to focus nor will it produce a data set that can reveal useful patterns.

Trying to watch too much too soon can also frustrate your efforts to build your observational skills. You will shortly start watching multiple individuals at once, intentionally focusing on the nature of their relationships. However, you don't want to spread your attention too thinly just yet. With fieldwork in general, the wider you cast your net, the shallower your data. Sometimes that's perfect. It can be exactly the kind of big-picture overview you need. Other times, it's going to give you the crudest outline when you could have acquired the means for the kind of wonderful character development essential for a memorable story.

If your attention shifted during this exercise, you may wish to try it again. Learning to attend to things more closely, to sustain your interest and be systematic in your observation work, also means being able to ignore things when you need to do so. Later on, when you're engaged in project research rather than pedagogical exercises, you may find a truly compelling reason to cast aside a day's mission to pursue something else. It happens and you'd be a fool not to pursue such an opportunity. But for now, far better to make a note and save new ideas for another day in the field.

In responding to these exercises, do not allow yourself to become anxiety-struck. I do not want you to feel overwhelmed or unanchored. This may be the first time you experience feelings along these lines. If you do, it's important to get this under control before continuing.

The research is undeniable: performance can plummet as anxiety and stress rise. The moment we start feeling overwhelmed and our confidence shaken, attention and energy is diverted from our ability to fruitfully apply ourselves to the task. Not only can we not perform to our potential under these circumstances, we cannot learn. A carefully controlled level of challenge—and an easy, self-forgiving attitude—can prevent this.

Remember Cziksentmihalyi's concept of flow, in which one becomes engrossed in a task and loses perception of time because the level of challenge in an interesting task meets or just slightly exceeds the level of skill we bring with us. For these exercises, flow is what we want. If you can't concentrate on what you're supposed to be doing because all you can think about is how you can't do it, then you need to pull back. Take some time to solve whatever the problems might be.

If the stuff you're carrying with you is getting in the way, take a few minutes and find a system to manage it. If you can't observe for two minutes and write things down before the next scheduled data point, then observe for only one minute. Or thirty seconds. If you're frantic to write the same information over and over, think about whether a template could make things easier. If yes, design and use it. If you can't write *and* photograph as you wanted to, put the camera—or notebook—away. Make the session manageable. Increase the level of challenge when you're ready. Of course, sometimes we do well by pushing ourselves with something that feels unmanageable at first. If you find that after a substantial period you're not getting to a point where things are under control, though, back off. You'll know when you're ready to step it up again.

If you felt frustrated and perhaps over-challenged with this exercise, you should also try this: take your responses to the first (open), second (focus on a body part), and third (individual activities) exercises. Place them on a table, side by side. I'll bet you see a huge difference in your work already.

Whenever you get frustrated by your progress, do this. It will remind you of how far you've come with what might be a very different approach to fieldwork for you. If this were easy, everyone would be doing it. Hardly anyone is, certainly not with the systematic, rigorous approach you're working to master right now. Every time you experience this frustration, take a deep breath, pull back, and also remind yourself that this is not about doing perfect fieldwork. It's about encountering the significant problems of doing good fieldwork and getting better at it. You may keep plugging away at this for a long time—maybe an entire career. Decide right now to not let frustration get the best of you.

Today's Write-Up

Speaking of frustration, patience, and making progress, let's turn to your write-up for this exercise. The writing process is getting what's in your head, out of your head. In your mind, one word can stand for pages of a remarkably detailed, complex collection of interrelated thoughts, emotions, and behaviors. Writing is about getting that on paper—and also challenging it and developing further thought and insight. Writing can be remarkably painful as well as rewarding, especially since ideas can be interrelated in convoluted, organic ways, and writing forces us to express that in a strictly linear, systematic fashion.

With that in mind, consider the writing task at hand. First, the form in which you take your data does not have to drive the form of your narrative. It could—sometimes it should—but it doesn't have to do so.

Let's say you produced a vertical timeline in your notes with the time of your data points down the left and your notes on what's going on at each time to the right. Essentially, you have created a chronological account of what you saw. You do not have to write up your field notes and present them in your report (or publishable paper, dissertation chapter, client briefing book, etc.) in this chronological fashion. You could. But you might instead choose to focus on sets of activities or relationship themes or a visible routine. You can go back, reanalyze your data, and do a new, different write-up as many times as you want, too, depending on what later becomes interesting to you. For now, best write-up practices include beginning with a tidy presentation of your data, but then you should feel free to present your notable insights however you wish.

In your write-up, watch out for the difference between statements like "Kwan lacks purpose" and "It appears that Kwan lacks purpose" or "It feels like Kwan lacks purpose." As researchers we want to be careful to stick with what we know we saw and not make leaps in our conclusions about it. Readers need to know that we are doing that too. Careful writing reflects a data-respectful mindfulness but also promotes it. We may hypothesize based on what we saw, but suppositions should be clearly indicated. Distinguish between the data, any claims based on the data, and any possibilities that may be further extrapolated from it.

This is one reason why I like observing another species—it makes it easier to notice when I report on what I actually saw and when I offer suppositions and reflections based on it. Any anthropomorphizing, for instance, is more immediately apparent than the thoughts, motives, and plans I might attribute to the people I observe.[3] Best practices in taking data and writing up, however, are the same regardless of the species under observation. Carefully distinguishing between what you observed (saw, heard, smelled, tasted, touched), and anything you impute about it will address this issue nicely.

Are you already a good writer? Do words come easily? Then think about becoming a *great* writer. Notice details and use them. "Kwan scratches his belly" is good. But what about this? "Massive yet nimble fingers form a temporarily rigid claw and Kwan scratches the fullness of his belly." It's over the top, to make my point, but you see what I mean. Close observation is the bedrock for original, more captivating descriptions. Whether they write their observations, paint them, perform them, or invent objects based on them, the greatest commentators on the human condition begin with the art of noticing and then conveying the closest of details.

Sociologists Howie Becker, Robert Emerson, and countless others admonish us, quite rightly, to give details in our field notes. Details about the duration, sequence, repetition, pulsation, and cyclicality of what we observe are no exception. Including this kind of data and the insights that can follow from it should be part of the gold standard for what it means to do excellent fieldwork.

Certain decisions about how we take data can make this more or less difficult. If you observe for too long a period before noting what you see, you will likely miss interesting details when you stop watching and take notes. You will be more likely to gloss over what happens, reporting at a superficial level that will not hold your own or a discerning reader's interest. In other words, you may well lose data before you have it—and your reader too. I'd rather read about thirty fabulously detailed seconds than four generic minutes of activity. As you try to find the right balance in how long to watch and how long to jot down your notes, don't forget that the quest for details should be an important part of your decision.

In your writing as well as your field notes, notice the ways you may have used specific knowledge familiar to you but perhaps not to others. It's an interesting glimpse of the particular lens through which you view the world. Special knowledge is one of the gifts you bring to the craft of fieldwork and to the analysis of your observational data. In the field, it can be a great form of shorthand for you to remember later what you saw. In your write-up, it can create a more compelling story.

Consider this note: "He grabs the sole of his right foot with his right hand—'happy baby.'" If you're a yoga person, you won't need anything more to remember what that gorilla looked like at that moment. When you write it up, you may have to describe it in more detail for your readers, but that simply gives you an opportunity to make your observations more memorable. It's a description that stands a good chance of capturing their imagination—especially if you draw it for them.

Moving Forward

Let's conclude the discussion of this exercise by taking stock of how it's going with ten important factors. Keep working on these if you haven't yet resolved them.

1. Have you found a good pen, notebook, or writing solution? If it's not working well for you, change it up. It doesn't have to be fancy or expensive, just easy for you to use.

2. Do you have your fieldwork kit organized? Are you mobile, ready to move when you need to without having to worry about all your stuff? Take time now to do this if you haven't yet.

3. Are you spending enough time planning your subject, your precise observational mission, and your vantage point for executing each exercise? If you tend to launch into the exercise and then find that you've set yourself up for a bigger or more amorphous challenge than you wish you had, try taking a bit more time before the next one to think it through. An eager attitude is fantastic, but it can be worth the delay in your start time to plan ahead.

4. Are you finding a good position to see what you want to see in the field? Are you craning your neck or making do with an obstructed field of view because you don't want to cause a fuss or it's too much trouble to move? There are definitely times when you have to make do, but if you can and should be mobile to keep your eye on the prize, make sure you are.

5. Are you being careful not to make up anything in your field notes as well as in your write-up? If you impute something, be sure to note that in whatever convention works for you. Careful is as careful does when it comes to knowing what you saw—and what you didn't.

6. Are you looking for patterns, repetitions, sequences, and the like in your data? By the time you get back from the field and write up your notes, it's easy to run out of steam. Remember to follow through and look over your data for patterns and possibilities. The job doesn't end with collecting and nicely presenting what was in your notes. Finding the bigger picture is an important point of this work.

7. Gathering data is your number one priority in the field. But if you have time, remember to take careful note of all the ques-

tions you have about what you see and where you are. It's likely that each question could serve as a separate mission for a given day in the field. As you observe, you will naturally develop a more finely tuned field research agenda this way, as one observation or insight leads to the acquisition of the next.

8. Don't forget to keep trying different things as you work through each exercise—possibly multiple times. What does it feel like to go super-detailed, ultra-micro in describing something? To not take any notes at all? To type your field notes on a laptop? To dictate your notes to a recording device and transcribe them afterward? To close your eyes and only listen and smell for an entire session? To only take photos or to only sketch for notes? Now is the time to experiment.

9. Earlier, I recommended appending a scanned copy of your notes to each of your exercise reports, so you can readily reference them and easily compare your field notes and the forms they take when you write them up. Have you followed through on this? I hope so, as there is another very good reason to do so. As a fieldworker, your notebook can be your lifeline. Imagine what would happen if you lost it. If it's possible to do so, always keep a digital copy as a backup. It's good common sense. (Note that in future projects, you may need to follow IRB-approved security measures for both your electronic copy and your physical notebook.)

10. Are you taking the time to look over your notes as a window into your fieldworker's soul? What are you learning about yourself, about what you are drawn to, and how you categorize the world? What kinds of information do you capture with different languages, techniques, and mindsets? Are your notes fairly homogeneous in tone or are there things you get excited about and caught up in—or for which you are bored out of your mind? Do your notes feel too few and too cryptic? Too many and too fussy? What would

you like to keep the same and what would you like to change about your note-taking process? Follow through in analyzing your notes as data about yourself, as a fieldworker. Look for these kinds of patterns and insights after every exercise.

If you were lucky enough to be working side by side with someone else for this exercise and you haven't done so yet, here's a fun thing to do: compare notes. Especially if you were watching the same individual for the same period, this can be quite revealing of how differently we may operationalize the same mission / exercise. It also can provide even more food for thought about things you might want to try if you do this exercise again.

If you would like to look at some sample responses to this exercise, they are available at http://global.oup.com/us/watchingclosely.

Notes

1. The earliest forays into time-motion studies paid a great deal of attention to duration, of course, putting that information to a rather soul-crushing purpose. We need not emulate the outcome of their work, but paying that close attention to precisely when and how something happens, including how long it takes to do so, is exactly what we should be after here.

2. This is a different decision when you're doing fieldwork for a project as opposed to learning about the data-taking process. When you're doing these exercises, you may decide that things are simply too slow for you to be able to get a grasp on everything you would need to do when the pace is faster. You may need to move to a different temporal or spatial location or pick a different subject and field site if you think that's the case. When you're starting out, you want a good match between the challenge at hand and your skillset from a purely technical perspective. Just be sure you give your chosen time, place, and subject at least one entire observation session as planned before deciding to switch to something else.

3. In general, I think that worries about anthropomorphizing when we study other species are legitimate but that these worries can sometimes work against us, too. They can prevent us from furthering our knowledge of and respect for other species especially if they prevent us from capitalizing on ways of thinking and being that we might actually share with them. This is especially true with other primates. To prevent the negative side effects of supposing other species

are like us, I think the trick is to focus on carefully discerning how *they* are, themselves, and, only after that—and with a good deal of skepticism—finding the ways in which we are like them. This privileges both careful data and the other species' ways of being while still allowing commonalties between us to become apparent.

Exercise Four—
Spatio-Temporal Mapping I

This exercise adds the dimension of space onto that of time. I ask you to focus on an individual as your unit of analysis and to note patterns in the cushion of space separating that individual from others. To prepare, we should think about the meanings of space—in this case, of proximity—for social beings.

In anthropologist Edward Hall's brilliant book, *The Hidden Dimension*, we learn that space—or, rather, spacing—is a form of communication demonstrated by every species, constantly used yet rarely consciously noticed. The book is a must-read for any fieldworker.[1] Based on the circumstances in which we are raised, we acquire different expectations regarding how much space should be between us in different situations. We adjust our proximity to each other given our agendas, relationships, and the sociophysical environment. Just as our proximity communicates certain things to others, their proximity provides important clues to us regarding who they are and what they are about. As with all social norms, violations of these expectations highlight them and reveal striking differences between cultures.

The amount of space between individuals provides a great way to think about the nature of their relationship. If we think of the individuals as the positive space, it's the negative space between them that gives essential clues about how those individuals are tied together at any given moment. Relationships are performed, after all, and they are performed over time and space. The space between us is at least partly a function of our relationship to one another plus the normative expectations for how we should perform that relationship at that time, in that place.

Of course, we see a mere snapshot of individuals' lives at any given moment of observation. The fullness of a relationship is revealed over a much longer time frame. A professor might go to a concert given by her husband, for instance, and sit in one of the theater's box seats at what Hall calls the "far phase" of "public distance" (i.e., 25 feet or more) from him. Yet afterward, they might stand close enough to each other to touch, within what Hall calls the "close phase" of "intimate distance." In both moments, our hypothetical couple is performing their multifaceted relationship across time and place, manifested in the spatial distance between them. We might come up with very different ideas of their connectedness if we were limited to either of these data points. One would need multiple, on-going proximity data points to reveal the complete picture of their relationship.

We might gain further insight about this social unit if we also noted what kinds of interactions transpired during each data point. With our and other species, proximity alone does not reveal the precise nature of what's going on. Intimate space is the distance for some radically different behaviors, such as fighting, plotting, grooming, nurturing, and seducing. It can be difficult to figure out just by watching if people are teasing or tormenting, playing, or fighting—and the precise moment in which one turns into the other. That seems to be the case for many species. Nonetheless, observing spacing over time is an excellent means available to any fieldworker who wants to begin figuring out how individuals might be in relationship to each other.

Hall reminds us of an important qualifier, namely, that all species seem to have a baseline of required, critical distances to be maintained between them. Hall provides numerous examples of what can go wrong if basic distance needs are not maintained for protracted periods. Rats become extremely antisocial—either highly aggressive or withdrawn and unable to thrive—when subjected to the stress of living in overly dense circumstances. Herding species, on the other hand, may get sick and die if they are not in direct physical contact with each other.

The current situation of certain of the big cats reminds us of the importance of observing spacing over time in order to understand more about relationships. Many species of the big cats live alone nearly their entire adult lives. One obvious exception to their normally solitary existence is the period in which a mother gestates, gives birth, then nurses and socializes her cub(s) to maturity. Throughout this process, we see great variation on the distances that would otherwise be maintained between members of this species. In humans, too, the amount of space that we expect to see between a mother and a child differs over the life course, as the child grows from fetus to infant, toddler, juvenile, teenager, emancipated adult, and, perhaps, parent.

Moreover, there are group-level and individual variations on these expected distances. Different cultures have different normative spatial buffers. City dwellers have different expectations from those living in rural lands. Families have variations too. People who stand "too close" when they talk to us and those who are literally "stand-offish" both violate internalized norms of proximity.

Expectations regarding territory appear in other social settings. What some people think constitutes their territory may be significantly larger than what others think is appropriate. Some individuals either purchase or are given larger territories than the rest of us, including those who occupy first-class airplane seats, mansions, and corner offices. There are those who sprawl over as much turf as they can, using their stuff and their stretched-out arms and legs—consciously or not—to take up more space than is normally allocated per person. Individuals may have unique tolerances, preferences, and a specific place in the social order, too, that manifest in the cushions of space we see between them.

Just as there are cross-cultural, cross-species, and individual variations on these expectations, other elements may mediate the distances we observe between individuals. The built environment exerts undeniable force on the amount and potential uses of space available to any individual. It may permit or insist on different distances between individuals than they would otherwise assume. Just as a given number of molecules become more and less compact depending on the size of the container they're in, so do people largely adjust to the space—and specific features of that space—that contains them.

Now, let's turn this kind of attention to the space between whichever individuals you have chosen to study and see what may be learned from it.

Today's Exercise

Spatio-temporal Mapping I: Observe an individual. Create a spatio-temporal map of that individual's movements that focuses on the individual's relationship to the other individuals in the environment. What rules appear to guide how much of a cushion of space the individual keeps around her- or himself under different circumstances (e.g., with different individuals, in different parts of the habitat, or during different activities)?

The trick to this exercise is to focus on the negative space between the bodies you are watching. You want to find a way to quickly note where your individual is each time you take data and also to note how close they are to anyone around them.

You can simplify this for the purposes of learning the technique by selecting only one individual to track in addition to your chosen subject and noting only where this individual is relative to your chosen subject at each data point.

If you are a precocious fieldworker, you may wish to also find a way to quickly indicate what kind of activity your subject is engaged in at each data point, possibly even noting the activities of any other individuals you are tracking.

Whatever you decide, don't forget to (1) appropriately benchmark your observations according to the time they happen (you might try every three minutes and see how that goes); (2) stay focused on watching the space between the individual you selected and the others in the habitat; and (3) gather duration data on how long a given buffer of space is maintained whenever you can.

I recommend that you do not read further until you have completed the exercise and your report.

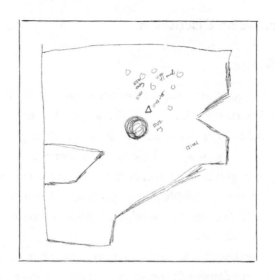

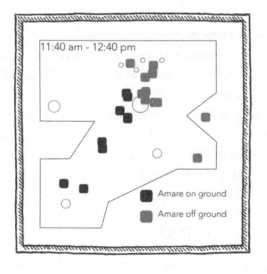

Post-Exercise Discussion

The Concept

With this exercise, you mapped an individual's proximity to other individuals across the duration of the session. For an exercise like this, we could add or substitute a focus on an individual's proximity to anything else as well—to objects, to food or water, to helpful, influential, or powerful people, or to any other valuable resource. We could map any individual's proximity across time to any category of thing. We could even begin to think of virtual proximity and how to map that.

As you reviewed your data for this exercise, I hope you kept in mind some fundamentals regarding proximity. In normal circumstances, the buffer of space we have around us is directly affected by (1) membership in a certain species, (2) location in a specific kind of habitat, (3) possession of unique individual tolerances or preferences, and (4) possession of a specific place in the social order. All of this informs and is informed by (5) the specific relationships and interactions that an individual has in any co-occupied (physical or virtual) space, which further influence that individual's proximity to anyone and anything else found there. For an enterprising fieldworker, the spatial buffer around an individual serves as an endlessly interesting entry point into any of these matters.[2]

The Mechanics of This Exercise

Merging attention to time and space in the field presents significant challenges. Finding ways to simultaneously take data on both dimensions and then re-present it in an intelligible way can require a good deal of experimentation. Fieldworkers who master this will find it a powerful tool.

Judging distance can be very difficult at the start. It is important to develop the ability to approximate distances. If you discovered that you're not very good at it, it's time to start practicing.

Find a retractable measuring tape and carry it with you. Whenever you can, as often as you can, quiz yourself about how far things are from each other and then measure the actual distance. Some people measure their thumb, hand width, the length of their forearm, and the length of their pace and then use these to check approximate distances. Play the "how far apart are those things" game with another researcher who is also trying to acquire this skill.

Watch out for unevenness in this skill related to scale. Some people's life experiences make them very good at judging larger distances while others excel at estimating smaller ones. If you're good at one and not the other you might want to learn to eyeball those kinds of distances too. Versatility is the name of the game.

More on Mechanics—and the Write-Up

Did you stay focused on proximity as you collected the data and during your write-up? As we saw in Exercise 1, students' baseline focus of attention tends to be, first, on the activity they see, and then second (maybe), on the location in which the activity is happening. It can be a challenge to maintain one's attention on the distance between individuals, rather than on their activities and location in space.

In fact, for this exercise, you don't *have* to collect data on location, although some students use this to reconstruct proximities afterward. At each interval, they note individuals' locations on a quickly sketched map or using a labeling system that represents different positions. They then estimate the distances between these locations and reconstruct proximities at each data point. It's a good solution to the problem, but you have to remember that the point is to calculate proximities. The exercise is not about mapping the locations of individuals. It's about mapping the amount of space between them.

Were you able to invent a spatial equivalent for "counting Mississippis" while doing this exercise? I am a baker and a sewer. As a result, I am good at approximating minutes and seconds and anything from a couple yards down to an eighth of an inch. For larger distances, I have to estimate using what's at hand, again using my experience to help. At five feet tall, I have a very good sense of how tall other people are relative to me. So, I look for someone nearby who is about six feet tall (let's call him Joe) and use him like a mental yardstick to visualize "how many Joes" this would be, if I either stacked him on top of himself, or laid him on the floor, end to end. A rapid change of proximity over a larger distance means that I am probably going to have to note the beginning and ending locations—probably while counting Mississippis—and then reconstruct proximity over time, afterward. Fieldworkers have to use whatever is available to get the information we need, or our best approximation of it.

It may seem an obvious point, but your data and your write-up for this exercise should be filled with spatial units as well as temporal ones. Inches, feet, and yards, centimeters and meters are the spatial equivalents of seconds, minutes, and hours. These common units of measurement have shared meaning and immediately communicate solid information to a broad segment of the world's population. Proximity is measured and communicated using these units. Your report should be riddled with them.

Other, much bigger issues also commonly emerge after tackling this exercise. They also have to do with the challenge of collecting and reporting on spatio-temporal data, but at a higher level. This challenge is only going to get worse with the next exercise, so now is a good time to discuss (1) effective ways of collecting this kind of data, (2) how detailed and painstaking we might want to make the data-collection process, and (3) how we might wish to re-present our data to others, given the specific goals of our write-ups.

Effective Data Collection: Templates

Templates can be important tools for your data-collection process. If you haven't already done so, start thinking about how to design and use them on a regular basis. A mission like Exercise 4 quickly reveals the remarkable advantages of developing templates for taking your data.

In this exercise, students generally adopt one of two approaches. After defining their subject and what buffer zone to measure (i.e., between this individual and X) the first approach involves using words and numbers to describe the amount of negative space at each data point and, usually, the location of the individual(s) and what she/he/they are doing. The second approach involves doing this but also using a sketch of the space—usually redrawn multiple times—to capture the data, especially the individual's location across time.

The second approach also typically includes sketches of particular behaviors and gestures from the researcher's field notes that better capture and help the researcher understand how the subject engages with something. Students of either propensity often take photos to supplement their written or drawn data. Like line drawings, photos can be extremely effective mnemonic and communication devices. But remember that neither a sketch nor a photo is an analytical point, and a group of photos and sketches does not constitute an analysis. They are ways of capturing or documenting data. They support and can be the focus of one's analysis, but they are not a substitute for it.

Exercise 6 will probably make you want to try this second approach if you haven't already done so. Begin by sketching the layout of the space you are watching. You then have several choices. You may wish to label different parts of the layout so you can easily refer to a specific location in your notes. You may wish to record multiple data points directly onto your sketch, finding a way to do so that lets you note the time of each data point and possibly how long an activity was sustained. A third option is to keep redrawing the layout throughout your session so that you have a blank schematic on which you can note your data at each interval.

A template makes capturing data easier and more systematic. It can be a chart that you quickly construct in your notebook, predetermining your horizontal and vertical axis variables and any columns and rows in accordance with the kind of data you want to take. It can be a vertical time line, with your data interval and collection times clearly laid out with room for your handwritten notes on the side. A template can also mean something like I've just described—an approximate sketch of the space you're studying, that you use over and over again. A template can be anything you wish it to be, then, ranging from the briefest of charts or tables to a sketch, photograph, or a complex, multiview model that you develop and reproduce, using a fresh (digital or hard) copy to indicate location each time you take data. The key to any template's success lies in how easily you can use it in the heat of a fieldwork moment.

Here, for instance, Jennifer Sculley (see figure 4.1) provides us with an example of a template she came up with while doing this exercise. Simple and effective, this zigzagging line represents a bird's eye view of the front of the gorilla habitat, which was designed to accommodate gorillas' preferences for corners over long, flat walls. She quickly redrew this single line for each data-collection point, indicating individuals' locations by their initials. Variations in vertical locations were indicated by boxes around their initials, as well as by written reminders. For example, at 11:00, a top-down

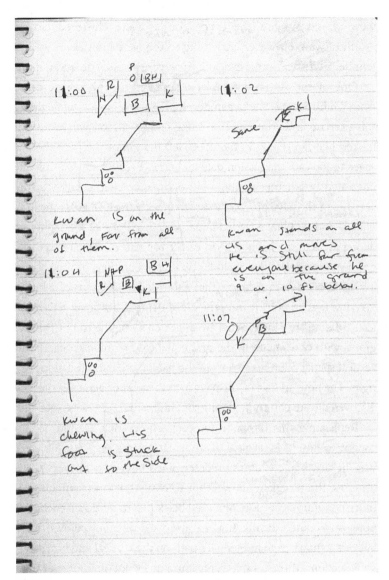

Figure 4.1. Jennifer Sculley's Simple and Effective Template for Spatio-temporal Mapping I

view would suggest the other gorillas were clustered closely around Kwan. However, according to the boxed initials as well as Jennifer's written note, vertically, they were actually quite far apart.

One of the cleverest templates designed for this course came from Chiho Sasaki. She began developing the template while doing this exercise and continued to refine it over several weeks until it looked like figure 4.2. In the upper left margin of the page there is space to indicate the session date and time. Because she was initially interested in whether lighting and occupancy were correlated, the very top of the page provides a way to quickly track whether the individual—indicated by a circled initial—occupied one of the lighter or darker areas in the habitat. Most of the top half of the page is a diagram-style template that includes two representations of the habitat, a straight-on view and, below this, a four-square diagram of a bird's-eye view used to quickly trace the movements of her agile, active subjects. Minute-long increments are indicated along the top of the diagram, with one square in the grid equal to one minute. Significant vertical spatial reference points in the habitat are indicated along the right. The bottom half of the page includes a list of activities that she discovered were common among the chimpanzees she was watching.

Replicating this template for each observation session, Chiho used it to note a great deal of information in a very fast, efficient way. In fact, while Chiho's predetermined interval was every three minutes, the template allowed her to easily track movements in a more continuous fashion. She used black pen to jot down each data point and related details. But she also used different colored highlighters to mark each individual's path on the vertical and bird's-eye-view sections of the template, putting a quick dot of color over their initial, whenever she noted their activities on the chart below. This let her instantly capture how each individual moved relative to the other along with what was happening at a given time. You can see the color version of this chart in the online materials for Exercise 4.

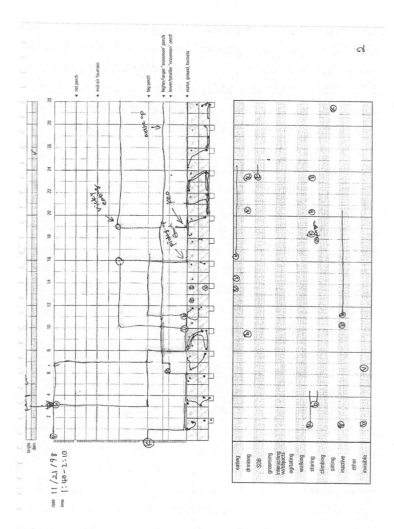

Figure 4.2. Chiho Sasaki's Fully Developed, Extraordinary Template, Final Version

For instance, at the start of the session documented by this page, V (Vicky) was at the highest point of the habitat. K (Keo) was on the big perch. At the second-minute mark, Keo dropped down to the floor of the habitat while Vicky stayed above. Chiho used her green highlighter (representing Keo) to trace over the black pen line that indicated his simultaneous movement from the middle back of the habitat to a place just forward and right. At this point, Chiho made two additional dots in the bird's-eye-view square. She probably had just noticed Kibali in the observation nook, high up next to Vicky. Kibali's location was indicated by a dot of yellow highlighter over the black pen dot that represented her. Vicky, traced by orange highlighter, remained at the habitat's top front right until minute 7, when she dropped down and moved to the back left, near Keo.

Whatever its form, a template should be something into which you can quickly add your data and that simultaneously reminds you of all the data that you want to take, each time you're supposed to do so. If you've designed and used it well, a template can also make it much easier to analyze your data. The cleaner and more visual your template is, the more it will almost analyze your data for you, as did Chiho's. It also makes it possible to easily combine the data in different ways to answer other questions later.

Templates provide an advantage in writing your report or, for future projects, the fully fleshed out notes and the papers, books, slides, and briefs based on them. A narrative written about your data points can create a flowing, continuous sense of time and better convey the overall sense of what was happening. It is a traditional form of storytelling and appeals for that reason.

Moreover, presenting raw data points in template form not only allows you to engage and understand the data in a more direct, immediate way, it also allows the reader to do so. In fact, it almost challenges readers to do so. In one sense, presenting the data in this form says to the reader, "This is *data*. It is evidence, collected in a systematic way." That can be useful to you as well as to your reader. It can serve as a reminder to everyone of what you're doing and how critically everyone should be thinking about what you've written.

In sum, templates can help us collect our data faster. They can help us present it more effectively. And they can help us keep our scientific feet to the fire by reminding us of the difference between our data and our claims based on it. All of this means we should take every opportunity to work on our ability to envision and use templates in our fieldwork. The more complex the activity you are trying to capture, the more important this will be.

How Detailed and Painstaking Do You Want Your Data-Collection Process to Be?

Whether or not you use templates you should be thinking about how detailed, precise, and complex you want your data to be at the point of capture. This decision depends on your goals. Any given method or combination of methods for gathering data could be better than another, depending on how you want to use the results. The way we take and write down our data should reflect (a) the question that the data-collection process was designed to answer, (b) the likelihood of wanting to use the data at another time to answer another question, and (c) how much detail we may want to include in our write-up.

I'll start with the first issue. Let's say I decided to watch Kwan, the silverback gorilla currently in charge of Lincoln Park Zoo's family troop, and Rollie, now his favorite mate. When Rollie was the newest adult female to join Kwan's troop, many people asked, "How are Rollie and Kwan doing—are they getting along?" To answer this question, I might spend the day watching her, noting her proximity to Kwan, and whether there were signs of conflict/ aggression between them.

I could design a simple template that sets this up as a chart and use it throughout the day, quickly recording what I saw during each

	10:10:00– 10:10:10	10:12:00– 10:12:10	10:14:00– 10:14:10
Proximity to each other? (in feet)	12	16	20
Conflict/Aggression? Y/N	N	N	N

(Notes)

Figure 4.3. Simple Chart Template to Track Kwan and Rollie's behavior

ten-second observation period, at each data-collection moment (see figure 4.3).

A chart like this would make it easy to record the three pieces of information that I wanted at each interval: the time, the gorillas' proximity, and whether there were any signs of conflict. Here, for instance, we see that at 10:10, Kwan and Rollie were about twelve feet away from each other, and there was no sign of conflict.

Later, suppose I'm still studying daily troop life and I become interested in the specific activity of foraging for food. I might want to know how foraging occurs, its relative importance for the troop, for each member of the troop, the role it plays in their daily routines and activities, and whether or not foraging activity could be an entry point for new cognitive enrichment, increasing exercise, or addressing the specific dietary and health issues of a specific gorilla. This previous chart is not going to be especially useful for later research about foraging. If, however, in the process of studying whether or not Kwan and Rollie were getting along, I also took careful note of what each was doing at each data point—including how they were doing it and for how long—I might have captured useful data for answering this new question.

All it would have taken was to add another row at the bottom of my list of variables: "activity at present, including duration," and provide space to write details about it under each time stamp. Probably, I would also have needed to slow down the interval between each data point, decreasing the total number of data points. This would have let me spend time writing as much detail as possible about what I was seeing.

The result would have been a template and data that looked more like what you see in figure 4.4. This variation has additional, specific places to record what Kwan and Rollie were doing at each data point. At 10:10, we now see that not only were there no signs of conflict between them, but also that Kwan was foraging and eating, which he continued to do through the next data point. Making this one adjustment would have let me go back to this earlier episode—collected while trying to answer a different question—and repurpose the data to help answer my new question.

	10:10:00–10:10:10	10:12:00–10:12:10
Proximity to each other? (in feet)	12	16
Conflict / Aggression? Y / N	N	N
Activity at present (duration?)		
- Kwan	forage / eating	forage / eating (still) glancing at R
- Rollie	sitting (got up after ~30s)	in transit, moving to far corner, watching K while doing so
(Notes)		

Figure 4.4. Slightly More Elaborate Chart to Track Kwan and Rollie's Behavior

This is why so many researchers adopt the position, "If in doubt, and if you can, get the data!" Thinking this way can be a real benefit to a fieldworker. How might you collect your insights now so it will provide the biggest return later—possibly even when you're working on something different? It's a good question to ask yourself, whether or not you decide to collect this richer, broader data.

If you think you might want to use the data from a particular session again, you definitely want it at as granular a level as you can get it. In fact, I find that the earlier my students are in their projects, the more likely it is that the additional investment necessary for more detailed data is worth it. They often don't realize the actual, higher-level questions and patterns in which they are interested until they are farther along into their projects.

But taking more detailed data can be much more labor intensive and mentally exacting. You may decide that the question you're interested in doesn't need that level of detail to answer it and answer it well, that you will not be interested in any other questions about this site farther down the road, or that you would rather go get fresh data whenever you know you need it. If that's the case, give yourself permission to collect the less detailed version. Simply concentrate on getting the pared-down data as completely and consistently as you can.

Re-presenting Data to Others: The Art of Storytelling

The final factor affecting your decision about how detailed you want your data-collection process to be focuses on your plans for your write-up. It's good to have more detailed data when it lets you tell your story in a more compelling or impressive way. Details matter enormously in good storytelling. But again, more is not always better. Even if you do take detailed, repurposable data, you don't have to present it in microscopic form to your readers. You can choose to present a less detailed view if that lets you more effectively make your point. The art of storytelling includes walking a fine line between too little and too much detail. Ultimately, you must find a good balance on your own.

Scott McCloud (1994) makes this point beautifully in his fascinating book, *Understanding Comics*. Creators of comics face two notable decisions: (1) the appearance or visual style of their characters, and (2) how quickly they move the story along. Much of the appeal of comics and graphic novels is the way they invite readers to put themselves into the story. Comic illustrations range from stick figures to those more like Charlie Brown or Calvin and Hobbes to Marvel's fully fleshed out, buff superheroes. Each style of representing a character has its purpose, and part of that purpose is to help readers put themselves more—or less—into the story. The fewer the details—the less the character appears to be a fully three-dimensional realistically rendered human—the more we tend to see ourselves in what we read. Dilbert's adventures and realizations are our own; it's why they make us laugh and look forward to the next installment. Stan Lee's characters are real to us, though. The action is happening to them, not us, and that's why we can't wait to see what they'll do next.

Comic strip authors also must decide how much detail to include in each frame, as well as across the strip, page, or book full of frames. Readers expect, enjoy, and demand the right to fill in the gaps between whatever details the author provides at one moment and whatever else happens next. So, authors must provide enough context in each frame but not too much, and they must decide how much action is implied in the space of the gutter connecting the frames to the left and to the right of it. The trick is to get the amount of detail they give and the amount they withhold just right. This keeps their readers' attention and gets the readers to put their attention right where the author wants it. Spiderman and his nemesis may be fully fleshed out and very real in our minds, but it's only in our minds that their actions can take place, because we want so much to fill in the blanks and make it happen.

McCloud's book is one of the most thought-provoking I have read on the art of storytelling—of any kind. It captures the essence of some of the most important decisions that fieldworkers must make when it comes to the issue of how to re-present our data. How much detail will we provide—in fleshing out our characters, what happens to them, or the worlds in which they live? How do we find balance in letting our subjects be seen as specific individuals living in a certain time and place while also letting our readers see themselves in what happens? How do we find the right pace for our stories, moving them along in a compelling way? How do we keep our readers' attention, in other words, by giving enough information to paint a clear picture yet still leaving room for them to fill in the blanks? We tell different kinds of stories from McCloud, in different ways, but the structural elements of our stories are not so different at all. Judgment and skills are needed for this part of our job too.

A good part of the storytelling task is concerned with how we re-present our data to others. Re-presentational options could include diagrams, photos, sketches or line drawings, animations of any of these, audio recordings, audiovisual recordings, written descriptions, and quantitative summaries. Just as there are advantages and disadvantages to using different techniques for collecting data, there are advantages and disadvantages for using each of these techniques to re-present our data. Moreover, there are endless creative options for how it might be done within each form—ways that are more and less effective, inviting, powerful, or artistic given the nature of the data, the communication talents of the researcher, and the audience.

Zones of Boundary Play
North Beach, Chicago, IL

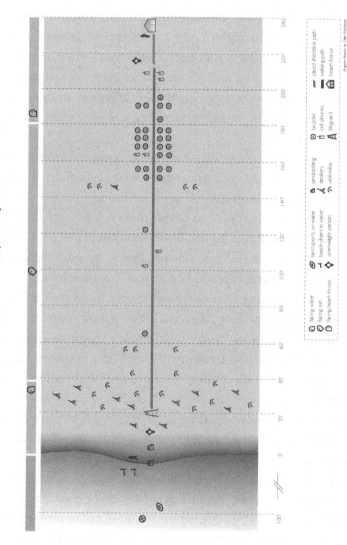

Figure 4.5. Gitte Jonsdatter's diagram, "Zones of Boundary Play"

Most of my students who have been trained in the humanities re-present their data primarily through words, which tend to be written in full sentences. Numbers occasionally slip in, although these are usually dates, times, and ages. Students trained in the natural sciences and engineering tend to use more numbers and often present them in the form of charts or other visual summaries. Social science students draw on both approaches. As my more qualitative students and I work together, though, numbers and numerical summaries, diagrams, and sketches begin to appear frequently in their work.

Design and architecture students use visual techniques most heavily to re-present their data, often creating beautiful, bold, computer-generated graphics in the process. (InDesign is their software of choice.) You don't have to be able to do this yourself. Using the data and rough sketch I produced one day at North Beach in Chicago while working on my book *Islands of Privacy*, the multitalented designer Gitte Jonsdatter produced a gem of a diagram for me.

I was developing a metaphor for the book based on "the beach" and was simultaneously interested in two related concepts—what I call "boundary work," and "boundary play." The book's introduction includes insights from my trips to Chicago's North Beach, including stories about the playful activities and conflicts I saw there plus an activity map of the beach. Following a conversation on the substantive points that I wanted to highlight regarding the hand-drawn map I had made in the field, Gitte made the following diagram. In the original (posted online with the Exercise 4 material) http://global.oup.com/us/watchingclosely material) she used blue to indicate the water (on the left) and yellow-green to represent sand (on the right). Following the tradition of the ingenious designer Edward Tufte (1990), the result is informationally dense yet compelling, far superior to any written description I might produce of what I'd seen.

A good diagram is self-explanatory, but don't forget that you can help your readers understand it by giving one or more examples of the information it conveys. For instance, the stroller and umbrella symbols on this diagram indicate the section of the beach closest to the water where families tend to congregate. They come early in the day, loaded with equipment and ready to closely supervise their children near the water. Helping the reader interpret what they see is part of best practices when one uses diagrams, charts, or figures to communicate findings.

Whatever your current repertoire for re-presenting your data, other options—and other ways of using those options—might be useful to you. As you experiment with different techniques, you will learn things about your data, your audience, and yourself. All of these circle back to influence how we conceive of data and collect it in the first place—especially spatio-temporal data.

Comments and sample responses to Exercise 4 may be found at http://global.oup.com/us/watchingclosely.

Notes

1. Some of Hall's book is dated and empirically unsubstantiated, a reflection of the time in which it was written. (If Hall had the advantage of the approach you're learning now, he probably would have qualified, if not omitted, a number of his empirical claims.) The book's focus on the language of proxemics and its most fundamental insights are still gold, however, and the questions it asks are as relevant as ever.
2. For further reading on proximity, try Robert Sommer's classic work, *Personal Space: The Behavioral Basis of Design* (1969).

Exercise Five—
Unstructured Observation

At this point, I recommend treating yourself to an unstructured observation session, with as little note-taking as you wish. Unstructured days allow us to relax and get more comfortable with our field site. More important, they provide an opportunity to step back and see the bigger picture. These days are great for connecting the dots we've already got and reflecting on the ones that might be missing, divining the next set of self-assigned missions.

Unstructured days also highlight the differences between these sessions and the concept-driven, data-oriented missions that are this book's focus. There are distinct challenges, advantages, and disadvantages associated with each approach. Mixing the two will help you learn more about when it might be best, tactically, to draw on either.

Both structured and unstructured observation sessions—and everything in-between—require us to make certain decisions about what we will do and how we will do it. Both types of sessions require us to come up with an intellectual agenda, a way to try to achieve it, a way to try to capture what we see, and a way to write up what we learn. With an unstructured approach, one consciously decides to be open to whatever draws one's attention, given one's intellectual sensitization to date, and to then do whatever seems to make sense as the day continues. The trick to an unstructured session is to adopt a wide-angle lens—at least initially—and allow oneself to think freely. Let whatever you see wash over you, focusing more closely as you wish on whatever seems to stick for however long it does.

You may do this, for instance, by planning where you initially intend to sit or stand and how you want to document what you see. The day could be spent journaling, doing only photography or only sketching, speaking quietly into a recorder—or a combination of all of these things. For your write-up, you might decide to do nothing more than distill whatever notes you have, in whatever form you have them, into a list of new insights or new missions for future sessions.

What's important is that you use unstructured days intentionally, at a specific time for a specific reason. This is not a mindless approach to the field, adopted by default. Rather, it is an approach selected from a variety of choices in how one could—and should—spend the day, carefully inserted into the sequence of more focused days because of the specific benefits unstructured days offer.

Exercise 5

Treat yourself to a completely unstructured observation session, with as little note-taking as you wish. Afterward, write the equivalent of a one- or two-page essay (or more, if you are enjoying the task) entitled "The Value of Unstructured versus Structured Observation." Include how you feel while you are engaged in each type of session as well as your thoughts on what the value of each might be, relative to the other, for you, personally. Think of this as the classic "compare and contrast" essay.

If you want, feel free to use lists or any other forms to capture and quickly summarize your thinking (cartoons, memes, a word cloud, etc.) since this is by, for, and about you.

The only point of this essay is to give yourself another opportunity to reflect on fieldwork, methods, your process, and what you're getting out of these exercises.

I recommend that you do not read further until you have completed this exercise, including the report based on your fieldwork.

When you have done so, a sample of other students' reflective essays may be found at http://global.oup.com/us/watchingclosely.

Structured vs. Unstructured Observation

If I were to choose between structured and unstructured for a project, I would base it on the research timeline and build in time for each. It would be nice to see what would happen when going back and forth between the two - I would imagine the rigor of structured (which requires more post- analysis) would balance nicely with the open-endedness of the unstructured (which requires more intuition in the moment).

Post-Exercise Discussion

About Today's Concept, Mechanics, and Write-Up

This exercise gives you a structured moment to realize that unstructured days in the field are perfect for reflecting on your process and your project. Because unstructured days often broaden the field on which we focus they can be perfect for thinking about *how* you are working as well as what you will work on next. They can reveal new ideas for collecting data, new concepts to focus on, and new missions through which you will pursue your ideas more specifically. They are also days in which you can forge new friendships or understand your place in the environment in a new way—or simply realize that you need to do both. On less structured days, let serendipity lead the way—be intentionally receptive to whatever might happen and wherever it may lead.

Did your unstructured day truly remain that way? Or did you wind up structuring a session for yourself, after all? If you did decide to use the time to answer a specific question (or two), what was it? What kind of data did you find yourself taking? How did you decide to do it?

Some students find the mission-directed approach so useful that in this exercise they quickly switch from letting their minds wander to focusing on something that they have been wishing to dwell on more systematically. Some focus on the goal of finally being able to tell their gorillas apart or creating a better map of the habitat for collecting location data, or being able to capture the duration of events more accurately. A focused session is preferred as it provides reassurance and helps them move toward an explicit goal in a way they might not have imagined prior to doing these exercises.

Other students stick with an unstructured session for the duration, then find their essay a welcome chance to reflect on the payoff for the new approach they are learning. Typically, the exercises in this book make students feel more pressured, but these mission-driven sessions help them acquire a different kind of data and think in a different way from that of a less structured approach. After Exercise 5, these students uniformly report feeling reinvigorated and ready to return to a more structured approach.

Remember that these exercises are practice, just like the exercises used to develop necessary muscles, techniques, and skills for other activities. We do them in order to level up. Eventually what we learn from these exercises becomes part of one's more seamless, intuitive performances whether in the ethnographic field or the studio, on the basketball court or the stage. People pursuing all kinds of activities engage in this kind of close work.

When it comes to the skills of direct observation, fieldworkers may not be used to this kind of practice, but it's the same idea. These exercises are designed to enhance your skill set. You're doing them to give you something to add to what you're already doing. The idea is to challenge your current way of working, to help you arrive at a different place, should you choose to do so. New ways of working often feel a little awkward until we begin to feel more in control of them—rather than the other way around.

Remember also that the goal of such exercises is not only to do different work, but better work. You should be able to go as micro or macro, as precise or as approximate as you want, focused as you wish on exactly what you wish, in exactly the way you wish. Using only a loosely structured approach may be more comfortable, but greater versatility, focus, and control can let you make other choices and realize things that you might otherwise miss.

It can also let you better communicate what you've learned to others. Think of your data set as the pages of a flip-book. The more realistic and detailed the image on each page is and the better it relates to the images before and after it, the more fluid and compelling the story can be. Vague, unfinished, out of proportion, or randomly ordered images will not tell an effective story. For the flip-book to work—and for the storytelling results of your observation work to be greater than the sum of its parts—you must pay attention to your data in a way that a more intuitive, free-flowing, unstructured approach to fieldwork may not permit.

Of course, the stories ethnographers tell are not based merely on temporally ordered, observation-based data. We use conversational data, experiential data, and theoretical and insightful snippets of all kinds to tell *our* stories. But if we want to get our *subjects'* stories right, we must capture them correctly. Only then can we properly interweave them with our own.

The first time I used a tape recorder in my interview work, I was struck by the difference between my notes on what people said and what they actually said. During the interviews, I had made brief notes while conversing. Mostly, I wrote swiftly in my car afterward, carefully adding to what I already had and summarizing what I thought were the most important, rock-solid insights. I then reviewed these first two stages of notes once I got home, inserting even more details.

Days later, I would load the tape in my transcribing equipment and revisit the conversation. Transcribing a taped conversation is a painful enterprise. However, I soon learned it was worth the effort. When I compared the transcript and my notes on the same conversation, I found that sometimes I was quite correct in the depictions that appeared in my notebook. But sometimes I had missed an important nuance, forgotten a critical qualifying exception, or left out entirely a beautiful, useful analogy that my conversant had raised.

These interviews were a minimum of one hour and usually two hours long. Of course I had missed things. As time went on and the project matured, I realized that if I had to rely only on my original notes to remember everything that people said, I would be missing many, significant points.

The conversation and note-writing afterward were organic and invigorating, much more so than the painful chore of transcribing tapes. But I was so glad that I did the transcriptions. Even if I choose not to use a recording today—for whatever practical reason—my interviews are better because of that experience. It has made me a better listener—and a better note-taker.

You might try doing a similar exercise but focused on observation-based data. For visual observation data, a video recording can provide the equivalent of a voice recording. If it matches your field of view and is of sufficient quality, a video recording can allow you to check your beliefs and notes about what you saw against a more objective record. Someday, you may wish to set up a video camera with a wide-angle view next to you, or wear a helmet with a Go-Pro camera on it. Test yourself against the recording by comparing the data you were able to capture live with what was recorded on the machine.

In fact, if you don't already do so, you may wish to rely selectively on video recordings to help gather and analyze your data. Smartphones and tablets allow today's fieldworkers the luxury of recording difficult sequences of action for later dissection. Eadweard Muybridge was one of the first photographers to analyze something the naked eye could not discern—the movements of a horse's gait. In the United States, as long as you are in public space or have the explicit (sometimes IRB-approved) permission of your subjects, you may find selective recording a wonderful tool to supplement what you are able to perceive on the fly.

In the field, we try to hear and see as much and as best as we can. Often what we hear and see confirms what we expect to perceive and the way we currently make sense of the world. Anything we can do to break up and break down the focus of our attention to make sure we are not glossing over or making up things is going to help.

The ability to quickly, intuitively make sense of what we see is an important one for fieldworkers. But so is our ability to look closely, to see what appears to be sensible, instantly readable flows of activity as individual frames in a specific sequence. The more time we spend now on the painstaking work of pulling apart and putting back together what we see, the more we will be able to trust our intuitive, organic sense of what is happening, later.

Exercise Six—
Spatio-Temporal Mapping II

Let's return to a more structured approach now with the second spatio-temporal mapping exercise. For many, this will be the most technically difficult exercise in this book. It should serve as an interesting counterpoint to your last spatio-temporal exercise, building on the techniques and insights you developed there.

Exercise 4 focused on space with the individual as the unit of the analysis. You selected a subject then mapped their movements and the buffer of space that they kept around them. The environment and the fixed objects within that space were at the background of our attention.

This time we'll forefront the environment, pushing the individuals into the background. The entire space, itself, is now your unit of analysis. Individuals are merely objects that move through it. We are looking for the ways the space constrains individuals' movements, overall, and the individuals' resulting use patterns of the space.

Here Is Your Challenge

Focus on the same environment as you did for Exercise 4. Create a spatio-temporal map of how the environment is used by all of its inhabitants. Create quadrants or use another (perhaps topographical) technique to break down the entire space into roughly comparable units. Observe and track movement through the space to see how it is used. Note timing, sequences, and durations of occupancy. It may be helpful to note the activity in which individuals are engaged at each data observation mark. Your goal is to watch how the space, itself, constrains the possibilities of how individuals use and move through it.

First priority: where is everyone at your observation mark? Second priority: for how long do they stay there? Third priority: what are they doing while they're there? If you can get all of this, you may be able to discern paths of movement or zones of transit versus places occupied for substantial durations, as well as clues to why individuals are where they are, given the activity they seem to be engaged in.

Think like a choreographer. Break the space into front, middle, and back (depth) areas as well as bottom, middle, top (vertical) and left, center, right (horizontal) zones. You may find yourself adapting the number of areas you try to track as the exercise continues, finding it easier to pinpoint individuals' locations across a different number of units.

Your focus here is strictly on the spatial possibilities of the environment and individuals' subsequent behaviors. Where do occupants spend their time? Where do they not? If you have activity data, noting the location of behaviors, then you might have a good clue as to why they spend their time in the space in the ways they do. Later, you could combine the insights from this week with those of Exercise 4 to create a fuller picture of why a specific individual goes where they go, when they go there, for however long they stay there.

Soft focus is the key to tracking multiple bodies through space. Think like someone at a busy intersection. Don't focus in on a single body, direction, or section of the space; try to watch the entire space the entire time. Allow individuals to come and go, move this way and that, as you try to merely receive—and possibly draw—the movement. Look for patterns of movement through the space, not the bodies making them, if that helps. Noting placements at each observation mark should be like taking a snapshot, indicating individuals' locations rapidly and automatically without really thinking about it. Once you have this, you can zero in on each individual's activity or whatever else you have time for. Be sure to reposition yourself as often as you need to in order to keep the entire field in view, according to whatever boundaries you've imposed around it.

I recommend that you do not read further until you have completed this exercise, including the report based on your fieldwork.

11:17 . from H₂ to D₂ vine . then up to D₃ ledge .

11:18 swings down vines to C₁ where she rests for 1 min then goes out .

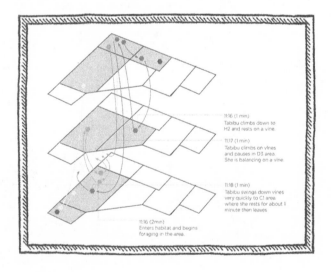

11:16 (1 min)
Tabibu climbs down to
H2 and rests on a vine.

11:17 (1 min)
Tabibu climbs on vines
and pauses in D3 area.
She is balancing on a vine.

11:18 (1 min)
Tabibu swings down vines
very quickly to C1 area
where she rests for about 1
minute then leaves.

11:16 (2min)
Enters habitat and begins
foraging in the area.

Post-Exercise Discussion

This exercise demonstrates the fourfold challenge of outstanding fieldwork: (1) developing an actionable conceptual agenda; (2) envisioning and capturing systematic, useful data that will let you explore that agenda; (3) analyzing the data to find useful and perhaps unexpected patterns and insights; and (4) re-presenting your data and analysis to others in effective ways.

On the Concept

This exercise paves the way for thinking about space as it is experienced, not only as it exists. Once we have solid data on the ways space is used, we can begin thinking about why that might be, and what it might mean about and for those we study as well as for ourselves. Our subjects each have a certain history and potential future within the space that we are observing. We, too, have a certain history and possible future with the spaces we observe, which influence how we think about that space and our subjects.

Yi-Fu Tuan is a cultural geographer who has written some of my favorite works on space, including *Space and Place: The Perspective of Experience* (2001). Here, he beautifully lays out his chief concern, namely, the ways in which people attach meaning to and organize space and place, and the ways in which culture affects and alters this. Tuan argues that three factors affect the experience of space:

(1) The biological facts.... The human body lies prone, or it is upright. Upright it has top and bottom, front and back, right and left. How are these bodily postures, divisions, and values extrapolated onto circumambient space?

(2) The relations of space and place. In experience, the meaning of space often merges with that of place. "Space" is more abstract

than "place." What begins as undifferentiated space becomes place as we get to know it better and endow it with value.... From the security and stability of place we are aware of the openness, freedom, and threat of space, and vice versa. Furthermore, if we think of space as that which allows movement, then place is pause; each pause in movement makes it possible for location to be transformed into place.

(3) The range of experience or knowledge. Experience can be direct and intimate, or it can be indirect and conceptual, mediated by symbols.... A longtime resident of Minneapolis knows the city, a cabdriver learns to find his way in it, a geographer studies Minneapolis and knows the city conceptually. These are three kinds of experiencing. One person may know a place intimately as well as conceptually. He can articulate ideas but he has difficulty expressing what he knows through his senses of touch, taste, smell, hearing, and even vision.

With regard to Tuan's first point, if we observe another species, say, gorillas, we realize they have physical attributes and capacities that we do not. As a result, they can move through space and interact with it in ways that will produce a different experience of it from that of a human observer. Differences in physicality within our own species also produce differences in how we experience—and design—space. Trapeze artists, dancers, and divers, as well as those whose physical attributes necessitate unusual or restricted mobility patterns, provide examples of how our experiences of space can be quite different based on our physical attributes and the ways we use them. Adult designers who put cameras on children's heads to design better environmental layouts for them have got the idea. The resulting video shows the kids' quite different fields of view and how they move through and relate to space.

In his second point, Tuan alludes to a distinction that runs throughout his book. For him, space refers to the unknown, the possible, the freedom of the frontier—as well as the danger and risk inherent to it. Place, on the other hand, is the known, the taken for granted, the comfortable and familiar, where the self is grounded in unique and persistent ways.

Any of our subjects may experience our chosen field as more of a place or a space. Depending on the size of the field, they may also alternate between moments of either, embedded in the broader experience. Think of the Great American Road Trip—where *places* such as familiar gas stations, restaurants, motels, and friends' and relatives' homes serve as destinations that dot the *space*—the adventure, freedom, and risk of the open highway—connecting them. Human and nonhuman animals everywhere seem to have place-like locations within larger, spacelike territories.[1]

Tuan's third point, like his first, addresses ways of knowing. Zoo gorillas, for instance—separated permanently from us in their own habitats—can touch, taste, smell, hear, and see things we cannot. Our species may have different cognitive frameworks that lead us to make sense of and therefore experience space differently too. Each individual subject and each individual researcher may understand space differently, depending on our unique reservoirs of space-related knowledge and experience and our possibilities of acquiring more of both.

Especially when we try to make sense of the spatial patterns we see in the field, we should challenge ourselves to layer Tuan's insights onto those that we already have. As we do these exercises, we should constantly remind ourselves that we study social beings, each of whom has a specific past and potential future with the space we observe. Our subjects have a relationship not only with each other, in other words, but also with the space that they share, however briefly.

As a fieldworker, you also have a relationship with that space. Your experience of it is inevitably different from that of each of the individuals you watch. Even if our field starts as space and slowly becomes place for us, it is likely to remain a very different kind of place than it is for any of our subjects. How might this influence your work? How might it influence your interpretation of the data?

You might robotically note that the low-status gorilla you're watching spends a lot of time under a certain log, for instance. One day, you realize that when your gorilla is under that log, he is fairly secluded from the other gorillas and suspect this is why he spends so much time there. You won't know from your present observations, though, if that space has comforting memories associated with it, which could be an additional reason he spends time there. What if this is where that gorilla's now-absent mother nursed him every afternoon for four years, and then curled up with him afterward to nap?

If you observe people at a mall food court, teenaged or senior regulars may have had all kinds of notable things happen to them there. The security guards, the servers, and cashiers at the counters, the workers bussing the tables, the women who stop by like clockwork each Friday after work to see what's been moved to the sale rack, kids in strollers or high chairs with their favorite treat in hand, out-of-towners shopping here for their first and last time—everyone you're watching experiences the space in a way that is influenced by their past experiences within it—and places like it. Their experience could be very different from that of the person standing next to them as well as from yours.

If you want to explore this idea more, imagine you are a writer and you decide to construct a novel, short story, or poem around the data you've gathered for this exercise. What emotions, motivations, and biographical histories could you invent for your subjects that would account for what you saw? Take what you've learned about the different locations, pathways, and objects of the space you just studied and see if you can invent a plausible past for your subjects that would result in your data.

For instance, having documented the one space your gorilla never seems to go, imagine why that might be. Could it be where he got cornered last year and beaten up by another? Could it be that he can't see his favorite keeper from there if she shows up? What if you've noticed that he always goes up high or hugs the window near the ground to get from here to there? Imagine why that might be. Could it be because of where the alpha male tends to sit and this is the only way to keep at least eight feet between them?

You can do this same exercise and think like an interior, landscape, or zoo exhibit designer rather than a novelist. Assume there is always a design reason—whether intentional or accidental—that individuals engage space the way they do. At a zoo, for instance, designers place heated rocks and air blowers near exhibit windows to encourage animals to display themselves there. Some surfaces might be easy for keepers to clean but hard on the inhabitants' joints or feet so the residents might avoid them. Visitors' pounding, staring, and yelling might make the inhabitants avoid other spaces. In short, what plausible, possibly interactive, *design* reasons might account for your data?

Finally, what anatomical, physical reasons might account for any given individual engaging with the space the way they do? Tuan's first point, remember, is about the physiological factors that influence the experience of space. Different physical capabilities lead people to adopt compensatory behaviors of which even they may be unaware. How could vision, strength, flexibility, size, and other factors lead to the use patterns you see?

This imaginative exercise can provide you with valuable insights. It reinforces the importance of remembering (1) that there may be very real reasons for the patterns of space use that you see in your field, even if those reasons are not immediately apparent to you, and (2) that subjects' experiences of space may differ not only from each other but also from our own. Our assumptions about—or obliviousness to—our subjects' experiences of space are definitely something to watch out for when interpreting spatial use data.

About the Mechanics of Today's Exercise

By now you have no doubt realized that quite a few factors influence your ability to see and accurately capture what is going on in the field. Among them are (1) how many focal points you're trying to keep track of, (2) your familiarity with each of your focal points, (3) how active your subjects are, (4) your ability to estimate distance and time, (5) how good your line of sight is, (6) how interested you are in what's happening, and (7) how much time it takes for you to note what you've seen. Any of these factors can make your job significantly harder, on any given day.

Whatever your mission for the day, if things get really crazy for you and you can't watch and write down everything you'd like to, you have several options. First, if it's a flurry of unexpected, chaotic activity, just watch, then do your best to record what you saw after things settle down. It's better to not miss what's happening than try to divide your attention between the field and your notebook.

Second, if it's a persistent, unexpectedly high level of activity, re-scope the problem. Trim it down to what you can handle. Follow only one or two subjects, not all of them; only this group, not that one too; only this part of the environment, not all of it.

A third option is to switch to soft focus, as you did for this exercise. Instead of trying to zoom in on the details of each component in the field, focus on getting the big picture instead. Zoom out and leave the close-up stuff for another day.

A fourth option is to set more reasonable intervals to take and record your data. Reduce the number of data points. Increase the amount of time you give yourself for documenting what you saw. Ramp it back up again if and when it makes sense to do so.

Fifth and finally, you might devise a better, shorthand way of noting what's happening. It is well worth the effort to do so for an exercise like this, for example. In fact, for this exercise, students usually use a variation on the data-capturing technique they began developing for Exercise 4. Any time you plan to gather a certain type of data for an extended period, consider developing a template that you tailor to perfection and then use over and over again. Ideally, your template will let you swiftly capture and analyze your data, effectively conveying the results to others.

Whichever tactic you take, the goal when things are overwhelming is to gain some control. Make the data-capturing problem more manageable, rather than put too much pressure on yourself. You don't want a hot mess at the end of the day. Simpler data, more carefully gathered, one day at a time, are a better choice.

On Today's Write-Up

This exercise on space encourages the most innovation in terms of how you re-present your data and write up your findings. As you'll recall, the write-up for Exercise 4 could be basically a list of distances. By focusing on the space itself, Exercise 6 requires you to develop a way of capturing and communicating three-dimensional movement through space using two-dimensional representations on paper. With gorillas—constantly adjusting their movements according to the movements of others—this can amount to trying to convey the moves of a three-dimensional chess game, where the players are the pieces.

Some students find it easiest to transform their data into visualizations of their subjects' movements, then use charts to summarize and analyze what they found. Others create only quantitative summaries of the data, with charts that show occupation and possibly activity patterns according to their designated quadrants. Summary maps indicating zones of use, disuse, and variation by individuals can be especially helpful in taking the data to its logical conclusion, making it easy for readers to understand.

The amount of work involved in creating computer-generated diagrams that capture this kind of information is significant. However, from a communication perspective, doing so can result in an extraordinarily effective presentation. It would take many, carefully written words to accurately describe this kind of data and findings—and sustained concentration from the reader to follow and develop a mental model of what the researcher is saying with all those words. More pictorial choices allow the data and findings to become far more accessible to everyone. The ability to create and use detailed, color-filled diagrams is thus an excellent addition to any fieldworker's toolkit.

Sample responses to this exercise, some extraordinary templates and diagrams, and comments about them may be found at http://global.oup.com/us/watchingclosely.

Note

1. See social psychologist Stanley Milgram's (2010 [1977]) maps of New York City and Paris, for instance.

Exercise Seven—
Power

After time and space, the next must-have concept for me is power. Over the years it has provided me with vital insights in my observation work. In this exercise, I use power to demonstrate how a fieldworker might take a concept less specifically field-based than time or space and use it in a way unique to the field. Instead of asking you to develop a new way of capturing data, I will ask you to work on what may be a new way of seeing data when it happens— as an example of a concept-related behavior.

Several decades in academia and a fair amount of time watching gorillas have only made me more convinced that to understand anything having to do with primates, you have to understand power. Its sister concept is status. Along with all of power's related concepts such as force, influence, and authority, they form part of the conceptual bedrock on which any fieldworker might build.

If you read just one work on power, make it Theodore Kemper's (2011) *Status, Power and Ritual Interaction*. This superb, interaction-based approach should be extremely useful for any fieldworker.[1] Building on the work of Goffman, Durkheim, and Collins, Kemper begins by focusing on status, which fundamentally drives human beings. We desire status. We work hard to get it and even harder to keep from losing it. The distribution, acquisition, and protection of status are what make our world go round. Status plays a prominent role in any interaction.

Like many social scientists, Kemper argues that status is scalar; we have a certain amount, which is more or less, and measured relative to another individual. In addition to this structural dimension, status also has a behavioral aspect. We express our actual (and desired) status to others through a wide range of actions. We confer or deny status to others constantly too, also through a rich variety of behaviors.

In a way, status expectations hold society together. They tell us whose will, whose interests, should be followed at any given time. We voluntarily submit to the will of those with higher status while downplaying (possibly not even noticing) the interests of those with lower status. The key is that we believe this is the correct and legitimate way to proceed in the world.[2]

Conflict occurs when parties disagree about their relative status and, therefore, whose interests should win the day. Now power enters the picture. It is closely tied to status in key ways. Both power and status are relative, both have structural and behavioral dimensions, and both are basic drivers of human interaction. For Kemper and many others, however, power is coercive. It is what we use to make others do our will. Status leads people to submit to another's will voluntarily. When status fails to get people what they want, however, they resort to power. Using physical, material, or psychological means, the more powerful insist that the less powerful do their will, in spite of any resistance.

Sociologists generally see power as having three forms: force, influence, and authority. Force is coercive and involves the actual or threatened use of power to get what one wants. Influence is the exercise of power through persuasion. Authority is institutionalized power, whereby individuals achieve their will by virtue of holding an office that is empowered by the people.

Here is Kemper's definition of status, which resonates with that of many other social scientists:

> Status is the rank or standing in amount of worth or prestige or other designation of merit and value that attaches to a person or social position in a group. . . . I define status also as the actual behavior or acts or means by which the scalar standing, worth, prestige, honor of a person or social position is conveyed in interaction. In this usage, status is *conferred* or *accorded* by these acts, behaviors and means, whether they are authentic or not. (3–14)

And his definition of power:

> Following Weber ([1922] 1946, 180), to have structural power is indicated by the likelihood of being able to realize one's own will or gain one's own interests *against the resistance of others* [sic]. (21)

> Like status, power is indicated by behavior. This comprises all conduct designed to overcome the opposition of others to realizing one's own will and gaining one's interests. (22)

Power can be observed, in other words, and Kemper describes some of its most basic expressions as follows:

> The ultimate here is killing the opponent who is blocking the way of the power-user's goal. Although killing may fail to obtain what is wanted from the victim, it often serves effectively as a warning to others who may be prone to defiance. Infliction of pain in any degree or incarceration or other restraint, or threat of these, are other standard physical means of breaking the will to resist.

... In the ordinary course of everyday life [however], power is most often exercised by psychological means, including withdrawal of status—attention, interest, concern, affection— or deprivation of valued material or symbolic goods and experiences. Failing to accord status when it is ordinarily due is a prime power tactic, such as ignoring, direct snubbing or pointedly insulting. Other noxious psychological means include shaking of fists, facial grimacing, raised voice, speech interruptions. Lies, deceit, and manipulation also fall within the power category, since they are intended to overcome the opposition of another actor. (22–23)

According to Kemper, all power is used to acquire or protect status. (In fact, he argues, we are driven more by the threat of losing status than by the promise of acquiring more.) In long run, however, one must find a way to turn power into status—into others' respect and recognition of our superior social standing. Otherwise, sooner or later, one's ability to impose one's will on others is bound to end.

Power, Kemper argues, is relatively inexpensive to use in the short term. If all you want is an immediate result, you may wield your superior power and get it. However, the use of force to achieve one's will has significant, negative, long-term consequences. If you want to stay in power, a leader must transform their power into (socially conferred) status.

This is because those subjected to power-based rule tend to resent it deeply. Those who rule by power will do so only until someone else with more power comes along and chooses to assert it. Those who rule because the group has conferred—and continues to confer—higher status upon them are far safer from contestation. Ruling is a much smoother process for respected, beloved leaders. They do not need to use coercive measures in the way that a merely powerful person does. Anyone who challenges a high status leader will find themselves facing the entire group as well, a far more formidable task.

For Kemper, status-claiming and status-conferring behaviors pervade all interactions. Power behaviors may or may not be present. While status behaviors will always be visible to a well-informed observer, only the *potential* for power-related behaviors is ever-present. Accordingly, Kemper argues that in any social interaction, four relational concerns come into play. Individuals focus on (1) getting status, (2) giving status, (3) managing their own power, and (4) managing others' power (26).

A fieldworker reading this kind of theoretical work should be thinking not only about the author's analysis but also how these definitions and claims might be manifested in visible behaviors. For instance, this last passage should have us wondering right away what "managing power" might look like. And how might we know if parties have successfully managed their own or another's power? Is managing power about preventing a visible expression of it? Is it about expressing power through carefully orchestrated displays? What would failure to manage one's own or another's power look like? Is it even possible to perceive the *management* of power solely through observation? Or would one need to employ other data-collection methods as well?

When adult female Bana joined silverback Kwan's troop, I witnessed adult female Rollie in what I would define as repeated incidents of managing Kwan's power.[3] Kwan's troop consisted of himself, his longtime female partner, Kowali, their son Amare, and relative newcomer Rollie, an extremely intelligent adult female who was raised by a savvy, powerful, and influential surrogate mother. At the time Bana appeared, Rollie ranked second of the two adult females, but my money was on her to one day surpass the then top-ranked Kowali. Kwan really, really liked Rollie. He was crushing on her from the start, constantly trying to impress her. That, in combination with Rollie's intelligence, boded well for her future.

Rollie also had a long history of championing underdogs and winning loyal friends among adult females and kids because of it. When Bana arrived, Rollie was true to form. She instantly appointed herself protector for this timid, passive female. Within weeks, Rollie forged an unbreakable bond with Bana, who, as the newest female in the troop, was at rock bottom of the hierarchy.

Time after time in those days, Kwan would get up from wherever he was, move very close to Bana, and begin to bristle. He would stand there, getting ready to lash out and discipline her—certainly not for anything she had done. Probably he simply wanted to make the point—to her, to the other females, to his son—that he was the boss and Bana was at the bottom of the ladder. It was his go-to move. Bored? Get Bana. Mad at someone else? Get Bana. Sun shining outside? Get Bana. He demonstrated his power—and her status—to everyone in the troop each time he did this.

Most of the time, Rollie would see it coming. She would swiftly move in and pass between Kwan and Bana, breaking Kwan's line of sight and deflecting his attention away from Bana. Usually, this was all Rollie needed to do to avert a bit of nastiness. It was just enough to get Kwan to calm down.

Sometimes, though, Rollie would have to make a second or third pass between them to break the tension. After doing so, she would occasionally circle around Kwan to his other side, sometimes assuming the flirtatious stance of a female gorilla offering to have sex. Given a choice, Kwan repeatedly chose to watch and interact with Rollie at these times rather than Bana. Rollie clearly used her influence over Kwan to deflect his attention so he would leave Bana alone.

In picking on Bana and in deferring to Rollie, Kwan constantly conferred status on each of his females. Bana's completely submissive actions and Rollie's interventions conferred status on Kwan too. Meanwhile, Rollie exerted her own form of power (influence) to manage Kwan's (force).

Other times, however, Rollie could not prevent an altercation, usually because she was elsewhere. Kwan would attack Bana. When this happened, Rollie would fly to the rescue. If Kwan was still at it when Rollie got to them, Rollie would launch herself at him with a fury and physical power that was more than his match. He would immediately release Bana, forced to now defend himself from Rollie. Rollie is half Kwan's size, but on these occasions she seemed fueled by justice, sisterhood, and adrenalin—and she seemed to always have the element of surprise. A keeper once described watching Rollie flip Kwan off Bana and onto his back, pinning him on the ground and biting him so hard and for so long that he sustained multiple, deep puncture wounds. In these instances, then, both Rollie and Kwan were engaged in expressions of pure physical, coercive power, as each tried to assert their will on the other. Their relative status—in each other's eyes as well as in the eyes of the other troop members—was undoubtedly affected by these incidents.

Their interactions serve not only as an excellent window into expressions of power and status, but also a fine reminder of Collins's (2004, 3) work on interaction ritual chains:

A theory of interaction ritual and interaction ritual chains is above all a theory of situations. It is a theory of momentary encounters among human bodies charged up with emotions and consciousness because they have gone through chains of previous encounters.

Gorillas, like people, are influenced by and producers of, chains of interactions. Any time a fieldworker watches what others do, when we try to capture a tiny, particular slice of their lives, we must remember that is precisely what it is—a moment with a history that led to it and a future that will stem from it.

Like a human, then, a gorilla's power is not simply a function of their physical capabilities. Intelligence and social acumen are other, vital sources of their ability to get things done despite others' resistance. The silverback may be the most physically powerful in the troop, for example, but a clever female may counteract his physical superiority in at least two ways. First, she can develop and then exert her influence over him. This can lead him to refrain from using his physical power against her and also to using his physical power on her behalf, protecting her and ensuring her relatively high status within the troop.

Second, a smart female can form a strong alliance with the other females in the troop. They will then be able to count on each other to band together and protect themselves if needed. If you've ever seen two or three adult females pounding and biting on a giant silverback all at once, you'll know that it's no problem for them to overpower and subdue him this way. It is precisely how the smaller females work together to keep the silverback from abusing his power and the authority they have granted to him, as leader of the troop. If this doesn't get him to straighten up and fly right, a female gorilla living in the wild will vote with her feet. She will leave this poor excuse of a mate behind and go find another silverback who knows what he's doing.

Other factors help account for the amount of power an individual might have. The social sciences have a rich literature devoted to the acquisition, nature, uses, abuses, and other behavioral manifestations of power. Machiavelli wrote a famous treatise on the subject, but there is lots of other compelling work, particularly when it focuses on unexpected influences on—and hidden expressions of—power.

Scholarly work about structural constraints on the acquisition of power fascinates me. Ivan Chase's (1991) research on vacancy chains, for instance, is a masterpiece of formal sociology. Power depends first on acquiring the resources we can then mobilize to impose our will on others. Yet Chase shows that what we have access to—the resources we can acquire—often depend on a tightly linked "chain" of resources, over whose availability and distribution we may have little control.

A soft-bellied hermit crab, for example, requires a shell—big enough to fit in and small enough to carry around comfortably—to survive. As it grows, the crab fills out the shell and must find a new, larger one. This is why hermit crabs constantly look for upgrades, seeking bigger shells to suit their longer-term needs. But the only way this can happen is if a larger shell becomes available. A vacancy must exist, in other words, to enable the crab to upgrade. Once that crab leaves its shell to take up occupancy in a larger one, its former shell becomes available to another crab, whose now-vacant shell becomes available to yet another, and so on and so on. A vacant shell that serves as an upgrade for one crab triggers a chain of vacancies, providing subsequent upgrades for many others.

For a hermit crab, the ability to grow means access to more food, more reproductive opportunities, and better defenses. All depend, first, on the ability to move into a larger shell. Thus, Methodist ministers, Manhattan apartment seekers, used-car buyers, and hermit crabs all demonstrate how the acquisition of power—the ability to mobilize resources and impose one's will on others—is constrained in ways one might not have imagined.[4]

Where a captive gorilla sits in the habitat, for example, brings together status, power, and vacancy chain behavior in intriguing ways. Power not only means having more resources; it means having the preferred versions of them. The hermit crab doesn't

just want a second shell; it wants a bigger shell. In fact, the more powerful possess and are entitled to the better of everything—larger seats that become beds on airplanes, luxury cars, mansions, tailored designer clothing.

The silverback, for instance, eats whatever he wants, first, taking it from others if he likes. He can have first pick of any cushy materials for his nest and he can choose the best spot in the habitat to build it. In fact, everyone else in the troop needs to get out of his way as soon as it's clear he wants to walk or sit wherever they are. This displacement behavior is the quickest way to discern one gorilla's status relative to another. Whoever has the lower status must get out of the way and give up their space to the gorilla who outranks them.

For captive gorillas, different locations within a habitat may be more and less preferable places to spend your time. Depending on the weather and one's present goals, the floor is generally desirable since food may be found there throughout the day. However, this is generally the silverback's domain. If he wants you to understand your low rank, he will not let you be on the ground whenever you wish. Moreover, you might want to actively avoid him if he seems to like picking on you. For both reasons, in habitats like those at Lincoln Park Zoo with good verticality, a low-status gorilla would want to be up high—and this is indeed where they are likely to be found.

There are times, however, when a low-status gorilla may have to give up her normally undesirable, high-up place of rest. In Chicago, this is mostly in the late fall and winter, when the highest spots in the habitat are also the warmest. Any higher-status female is entitled to displace her lesser from these normally less desirable places, and a lower-status female must then find a new place to rest. Should the silverback then also wish to enjoy the warmer air, the higher-status female might have to move too. She may then displace a lower-status female yet again, sending her to a third-best spot elsewhere. It truly is a three-dimensional chess game, where everyone behind the silverback must wait for a vacancy to appear in the next warmest location, behind whomever else has higher status—and more power.

Normally, gorillas voluntarily displace for each other throughout the day, according to rank. They know very well whom they can expect to move out of their way and for whom they must give way. But the hierarchy is constantly subject to change. For some gorillas, the acquisition of status seems to be their reason for getting up in the morning. They wait for every opportunity to whittle away at someone else's status and increase their own.

It is not unlike the dynamics that lead to office assignments in corporate America—or universities. The locations of both captive gorillas and office-working humans are influenced by status, power, and vacancy chain behavior. If we watch any of them, we will see these concepts in action. Both human office workers and gorillas essentially form an invisible queue for the next best spot, waiting to upgrade according to rank.

In fact, sociologist Barry Schwartz's work on queuing behavior is another favorite work on power. In *Queuing and Waiting* (1975), he links an intriguing range of behaviors, rules, and expectations to power. In the process, he illuminates another unexpected source— and hidden manifestation—of it.

According to Schwartz, the distribution of waiting time coincides with the distribution of power. He offers two sets of reasons for this. First, there are practical concerns: the more time one spends waiting, the less time one can spend doing other things. Second, there are the symbolic reasons that power and waiting are connected. Not having to wait, Schwartz argues, is part of "the immunity of the privileged" and the general rule that "power lets you modify the behavior of others and prevent your own behavior from being modified in any undesirable manner" (21–22). In fact, a "person can maintain and dramatize his worth by purposely causing another to wait," to the point where the imposition of waiting on others is actually an aggressive act, that is, a power move (34–37).

Accordingly, the more power someone has, the less time they spend waiting. This is true in a troop of gorillas, as well as for a group of humans. The silverback waits least while the lowliest member of the troop waits the most—for everything. Captive gorillas, however, must all wait for the keepers to open their doors, or begin their training sessions, a nod to the power hierarchy that crosses the walls of the habitat. When a silverback refuses to go through a door or begin a training session—or let anyone else in his family do so until he's good and ready—this is a similar, cross-species power move. By making the keepers wait for his cooperation, he's reminding them exactly who is in charge, at least on his side of the fence.

No matter what species you watch, no matter what research project you do, waiting—and therefore power—will be part of the behaviors you observe. Schwartz's work directly influenced some of my own early research on the gendered distribution of interruptions at home and at work. In "'Mommy, Mommy' or 'Excuse Me, Ma'am': Gender and Interruptions at Home and Work" (1993), I argue that interruptions reflect and reproduce gendered power relations. In this work, I view power from Steven Lukes's (1974) perspective—in which power includes the ability to impose one's will through agenda-setting and determining who will pay attention to what at any given time. The more powerful set the agenda; the less powerful follow it. Thus, the lower one's status, the more interruptions one will have, as one protects the status, time, space, and interests of others.

The gendered burden of interruptions, I argue, is achieved largely through the gendered allocation of more and less private time and space. This translates directly into more or less opportunity to enact one's personal agenda and achieve one's personal goals. For the employees I studied at a research laboratory, the gendered distribution of more public or private space and time at work and at home—as well as during liminal activities such as sleep, bathroom visits, and commutes—all demonstrated and contributed to women's relative lack of power as they bore the brunt of other people's interruptions.

These works tie in nicely with sociologist Lyn Lofland's (1998) review of the hidden yet visible ways in which the design of the built environment controls user behavior in general. In "Control by Design: The Architectural Assault on the Public Realm," Lofland turns her appreciation of the sophisticated social nature of the city to the ways in which the built environment can destroy the sociality that is a large part of the appeal of urban centers. Like Jane Jacobs before her—and many social scientists, urban planners, and architects since—Lofland bemoans the relative lack of attention given to the undeniable ways in which our environment (really, its designers) exert power over us. She argues that:

> Space *structures*—put parameters around—human interaction...by affecting (1) how interaction occurs, (2) who interacts with whom, and (3) the content of the interaction....The built environment certainly does not *determine* exactly how people are going to interact with one another, but it does amplify or constrain the range of interactional possibilities....The built environment is no more fully determinant of who interacts with whom than it is of how that interaction takes place, but it is also no less powerful as a facilitator or hindrance....We do not normally think of space or the built environment as a medium of communication, [either]. But...space not only structures how communication will occur and who will communicate, it also has consequences for the content of that communication. (181–186)

Lofland argues that between regulation and the design of the built environment, the latter is "most efficacious," exerting the most power in controlling the city population's behavior.

Good environmental designers, in other words, have the power to decrease conflict and minimize the need for individuals and groups to revert to the use of power in order to enjoy a good quality of life. For captive gorillas, good designers will provide multiple desirable locations high up in the habitat, in the midranges, and on the ground. There will be lots of paths for travel in horizontal, vertical, and diagonal directions. There will be plenty of nooks and crannies, where individuals can find a bit of privacy by breaking the otherwise constant lines of sight that can make everyone get on each other's nerves. Such features alone help keep fights and injuries to a minimum, as the designer's power minimizes the need for the gorillas to use theirs.

Now let's put all this theory and these many observations about power to work in whatever field you've chosen. For this exercise, think about what expressions of power might look like in your field, among your subjects. Remember, power is the ability to achieve one's will in spite of the resistance of others. It is coercive by nature and may be seen when one uses force, influence, and/or authority to impose one's wishes on another. Use the basic definition of power, its related concepts, and the examples of power that I've given you—plus any of your own insights—to look for visible instances of power in the field.

You may have to wait a while before you see it. It is easy to miss power maneuvers. What looks like the mundane act of an employee walking from one office to another, clicking a mouse, or texting on their cell phone could be the result of a more powerful person's insistence that they do so. One would need to be especially talented at reading an individual's body language to figure out how voluntary these acts were. It would be much easier to determine if these were the outcomes of power moves if we saw the initial resistance that led to the directives.

A fieldworker also may have difficulty perceiving the connections between different power moves because of the time frame in which we do our research. On a given day, we might witness an interaction in which a less powerful individual is humiliated and forced to submit to the more powerful individual's will. Yet this may be the very incident that leads the subordinate individual to depose that unwise wielder of power a year later.

The ways in which the built environment imposes the interests of those making the design decisions on those who use the environment also may not be obvious—in the short or the long run. Those not trained to think about the built environment may not be aware of the power plays they're seeing, the choices that were made, and those that were not. Yet it behooves any fieldworker to spend time thinking about how these decisions impose the interests of the design stakeholders on our subjects, too, so that the silence of the building, spaces, materials, floor plans, and layouts, even the styles and configurations of furniture, is not mistaken for an absence of its effects.

Today's Exercise

Today will be an extended, free-form observation session. Note when you begin and end your session, but do not restrict yourself to predetermined moments of observation. Today, you want to think with as much of the field as you possibly can, using whatever is available to think about expressions of power in the field. This is a different way to do concept-driven fieldwork. It's just as analytical but is not driven by the rhythms and restrictions of the interval research approach. Instead, you will look for things that you believe are related to your conceptual focal point—

power—and use them to think more about this concept and how it manifests in your subjects' lives.

Select one of the following two assignments. Don't forget to answer the question at the end.

Option I. Track any instances in which one individual seems to assert power over another. These may be seen (1) when a less powerful individual refrains from doing what they seem to want to do and/or changes what they are doing because of what another individual does, is doing, or wants to do. Such instances also include times when (2) a more powerful individual resists changing whatever they want to do, regardless of what the less powerful do or want to do, or might wish the more powerful would do.

Pay attention to what appear to be preferred or privileged spaces (e.g., perhaps any space occupied by the most powerful or perhaps specific locations in the environment) and times (e.g., a particular slot in the line-up; the longest or shortest duration of engaging in a certain activity or of possessing a certain object or space). Be sure to pay particular attention to any instances of waiting or interruption.

Does what you see resonate with, complicate, or challenge what you think you've already learned about the status hierarchy within this group?

Option II. Power is always relative. The distribution of power within the group or space you have been observing is framed by the distribution of power outside it too. Record instances in which you see a visible impact of the spatial (or temporal) design decisions present in your field on your subjects' behaviors. Think very high level here as well as down close, at the level of micro-interactions.

In other words, look for broad, generalized examples of the ways the designers of your subjects' lives support and control their users through the structures they provide. You can do this by looking for and reflecting on those generalized structures as well as by focusing on the micro-interactions between individuals enabled by those structures. Either entry point should get you to roughly the same analytic place.

How do these design decisions enable, even facilitate, the existing group hierarchy? What do more powerful individuals appear to need in order to achieve their goals, carry out their roles properly, and assert and maintain their position of higher status? What do less powerful individuals appear to need in order to achieve their goals and carry out their roles properly, given their positions in the hierarchy?

To be included in this week's reflection part of your report, whichever option you pick: If your goal was to disrupt your subjects' existing status hierarchy as much as possible, what single temporal or spatial feature of your field would you change? How would you change it?

I recommend that you do not read further until you have completed this exercise, including the report based on your fieldwork.

Umande + Amare Umande comes to sit up on the ledge
by the glass, facing out towards the gallery, and Amare
follows him soon after. He comes to rest close beside Umande
but without actually looking at him. They are probably
less than two feet apart from each other. Without looking
over, Umande reaches out and touches Amare's left hand
for a few seconds (less than ten). Being touched, Amare
looks over briefly, then makes a move to sit even closer to
Umande. Amare actually positions himself directly behind
Umande and tries to hug him from behind.

Post-Exercise Discussion

About This Concept

For this kind of exercise or mission, the more you do to educate yourself and think through the concept that you want to explore, the better your data will be. Whether you are interested in gender, generosity, mobility, kinship, truth, identity, efficiency, or any other concept, do your homework, first, outside of the field. You'll be better able to operationalize your concept, that is, envision a way to measure and carefully explore it, turning it into an actionable mission for the day.

I hope you saw something during the session that both challenged and clarified your understanding of power and how it works. I am delighted when things happen in the field that do not fit neatly into the categories and the analytical framework I brought with me that day. Stripping the concepts of power and status down to only what I can directly observe has helped me clarify both of them and the ways they infuse the most mundane of interactions and relationships.

About the Mechanics of This Exercise

Many students enjoy this exercise. Freedom from the constraints of interval research while focusing on an important concept results for them in a most satisfactory experience. Partly, this is because this exercise provides an opportunity to reflect and to start systematically connecting the dots regarding the relationships students have begun to perceive during the previous exercises. If you're studying a group that you don't yet understand, anything that helps you not only get more pieces to the puzzle but also start putting together the pieces you have can be extremely welcome.

Getting a sense of the social hierarchy, of each individual's status relative to others, of the ways in which players seem to be jockeying for—or accepting of—their current position can be vital information for understanding any field. It may be easier to see this in action while watching gorillas or another species, but once you see it in them, you will keep seeing it in people, too.

About the Write-Up

This exercise also reminds us of the circumstances in which it is vital that we document not only the data but also our thoughts on it while in the field. The more conceptual our data, the more illustrative it is, the more important it is that we find a way to jot down not just the data, per se, in the heat of the moment, but also the reasons we think this is data and why it might matter to us. When our self-appointed mission is to "look for examples of x," our data may take the form of a chronological list of things that we believe exemplified the concept x. However, we should put significant effort into writing down exactly how and why we think each item on the list is an example of this concept-in-action, lest we forget about it later on.

Do this additional documentation in the field, as much as possible, as well as later, when writing up your notes. Do not wait too long. It may be impossible to recall weeks afterwards what you were thinking when you collected your data and why this thing you saw made you think it was about your chosen concept. Instead, as close to the data-collection process as possible, write up all the careful thinking you did while (1) exploring the concept, itself, deciding how it might be manifested in the field; (2) getting your data, including why you think this concept played a central role in each of the instances you identified (either because the concept helped you realize what was going on or because the event clarified, challenged, and/or demonstrated the concept itself, etc.); and (3) looking back over the data later, in order to find any patterns or potential conclusions.

With this kind of work, we must put in the effort to systematically explain our scholarly interests, our data, and our subsequent conclusions *to ourselves*. This is not just a best (and obvious) practice. A concept-driven approach to fieldwork *requires* that you spend time carefully constructing a narrative that articulates exactly what you are interested in, the way this unfolded and was revealed during your fieldwork, and any conclusions—or possible conclusions—you've drawn based on this work. This process helps us think through what we are doing and why.

We also have to do this because we cannot assume anything about our readers' shared understanding of any part of our process. Because of the work we've done, our understanding of a concept may be different—likely better developed and more nuanced—than that of some readers. Moreover, our data may not look like any data they've seen or considered before. If we don't walk them through the process of how we got there, there's a good chance they will not accept our conclusions. When you do unusual and innovative work, and when you take the time to carefully explain why your assumptions, process, and conclusions are logical and useful, it's a surefire way to put your own stamp on the body of scholarship and practical work related to your interests.

Comments and sample responses to Exercise 7 may be found at http://global.oup.com/us/watchingclosely.

Notes

1. Pages 11–32 are an essential primer. If you have the time and inclination, you could turn next to the first three chapters of Randall Collins's (2004) work on interaction ritual chains, focusing especially on his analysis of power and status rituals.

2. In a society such as the United States, of course, there is a bottom line of common and equal legal/civil standing among individuals. There are situations in which

we acknowledge a given individual's—or the state's—higher/lower status than others, but there are other situations in which that individual—or even the state—is considered to have no more or no less status than anyone else. We grant others authority—limited, legitimated power—over us in some ways but reserve other realms in which we maintain equal or possibly even more status than they.

3. She was, of course, also managing his status, which, as Kemper argues elsewhere, permeates all interactions.

4. In *The Making of an Authoritarian Regime: Greece, 1944–1974* (1976), Kyriakos Kontopoulos showed how a small group of insurgents systematically used vacancy chains within the Greek army to place and promote themselves in the years leading up to their successful 1967 coup d'état. Through horizontal transfers and vertical promotions, they ensured that they would control key positions when they decided it was time to take over the government.

Exercise Eight—
Object Mapping I

Anyone with a special interest in objects (including fans of Bruno Latour's [2005] actor-network theory) will enjoy the next two exercises. Both offer another way to think with the field, by focusing on an object as the entry point. We will again leave interval research aside for this challenge in favor of more free-form observation.

For Exercise 8, you will select a single object and focus on it for the duration of the session. Select an object that you expect to be used at least a few times, but not one that will be in constant use. You should be looking at your object for a fair amount of time when nobody interacts with it.

This exercise challenges you, in part, not think of the downtime in which your object is "sitting still" and being ignored as boring, wasted time. For a fieldworker, this is valuable time, an opportunity to become lost in your object. Whenever you find your focus of attention is left alone, engage it as fully as you can. Observe so closely, reflect so deeply, that you see things and describe things about your object that you—or anyone else—might never notice otherwise. Take nothing about it for granted.

Drawing from the art world, begin with a formal analysis of your object. Describe it objectively and thoroughly, including its environmental context. Include shape, color, material, texture, size, placement, fixed/semi-fixed/unfixed, how it fits in to its surroundings.

What assumptions are embedded in the object's design, creation, and availability? Focus on assumptions about the users; other stakeholders; its intended uses and expected use patterns; the intended consequences and goals of making it available in this way; engineering constraints; aesthetic considerations; expectations for maintenance; likely fiscal constraints on its creation and use; the goals embedded in its design, availability, and use; and interesting alternatives for any of these that were not pursued but could have been, and so on. Throughout the session, take time to also reflect on anything you see that might constitute an *un*intended use, goal, consequence of your object, and inadvertent assumptions it might reflect.

Focus on the symbolic side of your object too. What do you think its value is to the individuals who interact with it? To those who don't? What does it mean to them? What do you think it might stand for—in general as well as in this field with these subjects at this time? What would happen if it were taken away? What if more of it were made available? Is there something you'd like to see in its place? Can you imagine how the apparent role of this object could be met by something else? Especially symbolically, what could take its place?

The possibilities are endless for where your mind might go with any time you have to muse on this thing. Include reflections like whether or not this is a special object, used rarely or with deep significance, or a common object, used frequently with little thought—until, perhaps, it fails. How vital is it that the object functions properly whenever it is needed? Is it a focus of competition, a sign of status, or an instrument of power? Does it play a role in maintaining the social structure and relationships between distinct groups or individuals within your field?

Consider also how your thoughts about this object changed over the course of the exercise. What did you think about this object before? How did your thoughts change while watching it?

You get as much out of quiet observation opportunities as you put into them. They are a Rorschach test for wisdom and imagination as a fieldworker. A mindset that mines the possibilities of every moment in the field will see these quiet moments as the gift they can be.

Today's Exercise

Observe and record the use of a particular inanimate object by the group you are studying. This can be a fixed feature of the environment or any other inanimate object.

Look at how the object is incorporated into the group's activities (or not). How often is it used and for how long? In what ways? By whom? How does it affect or constrain individuals' behaviors? What behaviors does it elicit or prevent? In your view, what functions does this object fulfill? (Make a list. Be specific, but think big picture, too. Vertically integrate your thinking about function, from the lowest, most pragmatic level up to the highest, most symbolic one.) Does your observation of this object give you any insight into the priorities and relationships of any individuals in the group?

Think of this assignment as "a day in the life of (this object)," where your constant focus is the object, regardless of who comes in and out of the picture around it.

If the object you have chosen remains unused after thirty minutes, you may wish to switch your attention to a different object, in order to get the most out of the exercise.

I recommend that you do not read further until you have completed this exercise, including the report based on your fieldwork.

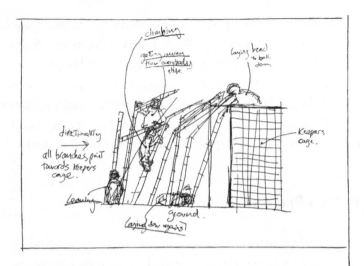

Figure 4.

Susie used it to protect herself and escape from all the other individuals, Kowali climbed up a stalk to go to the top of the keepers cage (figure 3), Bahati used it as a platform, a vantage point to assess the situation but for Kwan it acted more as an obstacle, not being able to move on the stalks and around them easily due to his size, he decided to avoid it altogether.

Post-Exercise Discussion

About Today's Concept

Focusing on an object can provide great insight into its users' lives. One could do this in many contexts. Focus on a kitchen counter to gain insight about the family, a coffee machine for employees, a tip jar for wait staff, a cell phone for a teenager, a handgrip on a subway train for commuters—almost anything can reveal useful facts to an interested (and interesting) ethnographer.

This is not only true for designers; the technique is also especially good for seeing variation in concepts and responses to situations, exactly what a sociological fieldworker needs to produce good, midrange theory. Sociologist Harvey Molotch sparkles at work like this. Read, for instance, his contributions to *Toilet* (2010, with Laura Noren), if you want to see best practices in how an object can provide an extraordinary entry point into thinking about forms, values, relationships, and the local political economy.

One can do variations on Exercise 8, of course. Shift the unit of analysis so that an individual (or group) becomes the focal point and map the individual's or group's day by focusing on the objects with which they interact. It becomes "a day in the life of this person" (or group) as seen through the objects they touch. The exercise could look something like this:

Select an individual. Map this individual's day and immediate foci of attention by mapping the objects she or he physically touches. Note all the objects she or he interacts with, including the duration, sequence, and cyclicality of these object-based interactions.

Once your session is over—but before you leave the field of view—reflect on the following: Are there any objects that were close at hand but ignored?

Why do you think that is? Is it, for instance, because the individual seemed uninterested in them, or did she or he seem to avoid them for other, especially social, reasons?

How important would you say each available object is in the day of this individual, based on the amount of time or the intensity with which they interacted—or tried to interact—with it?

Which objects, if any, were used especially to mediate the individual's interactions with other individuals? What role does each of these objects play, therefore, in the individual's relationship with other individuals? If you think of each object as an entry point into your subject's relationships, in other words, what does its use reveal about those relationships?

Overall, what can you tell about this individual from mapping the object-based interactions of their day?

When concept-based fieldwork is combined with the careful study of objects, the results can be profound. Layering an interest in time, space, power, or any other concept onto an interest in objects reveals insights and patterns we might not otherwise notice. One day, for instance, I was musing about Hall's concept of personal space—the focus of a lecture I was preparing. I was thinking about how one could visualize personal space, the fact that we learn about personal space, and that, even though we might be oblivious to it, these bubbles are an active presence around us as we negotiate the social and physical environment.

It was raining as I walked to the library later that week. I realized that watching people with umbrellas was the perfect way to visualize how personal space is a socialized practice. By the time I got to my destination, I'd seen a bunch of little kids with umbrellas walking to school. I was reminded that young children are clueless about personal space. This is why they constantly bump into other people and other things with their umbrellas.

In the library, I positioned myself by a window, took out my notebook, and continued watching. People entering and exiting cars or buildings while coordinating the opening and closing of umbrellas are excellent for thinking about personal space in liminal, private-public moments. The classic umbrella tilt of people passing each other on the sidewalk shows the constant, normally invisible negotiation of personal space in public, and how we temporarily condense our normal claims to it in narrow places. Big men with huge golf umbrellas taking up more than their fair share of the sidewalk—and getting dirty looks from other passersby—nicely reveal personal space expectations—as well as the informal consequences of their violation.

Another day, I was thinking about the concept of accessibility—musing on the norms of accessibility and the mundane objects and interactions in our daily lives that manifest (and assume) our expectations about who can and should access our things. I decided to explore this by doing a quick inventory of all the doors in my house. I noted the location of each door, whether or not there was a lock on it, whether the lock appeared to be built into the door or added afterward, whether or not the lock was routinely or rarely used and on what occasions, whether the door was expected to be opened freely by any or only some family members, whether the door was expected to be opened freely by guests and which ones, and finally, what the consequences might be of an unexpected person opening that door. From the front door, the back door, the refrigerator door, and the parent(s) bedroom door to the linen closet, and the liquor and medicine cabinet doors, to all the drawers that have what amount to "doors" on them, too, it is a fascinating exercise that could be conducted in any house. By looking at a single type of object and thinking about it across a given space, my activity and the chart I produced helped me gain a much richer understanding of the concept that interested me—as well as this previously taken-for-granted aspect of my home.

Sociologists are not as focused on objects as we should be. Anthropologists pay careful attention to material culture. Archeologists, architects, and, of course, designers set the standard. After this exercise, you may wish to build a more intentional focus on objects into your own repertoires of fieldwork if you think it would add to the richness of your research.

In my own work, I have long felt the gravitational pull of objects. In *Home and Work: Negotiating Boundaries Through Everyday Life* (1996), I looked carefully at the ways people conceive of the concepts home and work, in part by tracing the objects that appeared at different times and in different places throughout their days. During their trips between the spaces typically associated with home and work—residence, office, laboratory, machine shop—individuals shifted between different collections of objects and used still other "bridging" or "transitional" items and routines to help them do so. From the ways people managed their keys, calendars, clothes, and photographs to what they ate and drank, listened to, read, and spent—especially when and where they did these things—one could map an individual's conceptual framework as well as their day by noting the objects they routinely encountered and the ways in which they configured and used them.

More recently, I used objects to explore the concepts of privacy and what is "private" or "public." In *Islands of Privacy: Concealment and Disclosure in Everyday Life* (2010), I devoted a chapter to an inventory of people's wallets and purses and how they managed their privacy through these "identity kits." To understand how people thought of the concepts of "private" and "public," I asked interviewees to take all of the contents from these vessels and put them into two piles, one that was more private and another that was more public. I then asked them to explain why they put each item where they did—including a third, hybrid pile that sometimes appeared—and I tracked the classification of each type of item.

Along with my co-author on this chapter, Jay Melican, who has a PhD in design, I then delved into how individuals decided what went where. We found that people essentially asked themselves two questions when classifying an object, "Is this object personally meaningful to me?" and "Would it be bad for me or those for whom I am responsible if I lost control of this object?" The combined answer to both questions resulted in the object's classification as more private ("yes" and "yes") or more public ("no" and "no"). The classification of wallet and purse contents thus shows the categorical boundaries of private and public and how these concepts relate to each other. Through their selective concealment and disclosure, these contents also reveal how people think about—and actively try to manage—a third concept, that of privacy.

So did the objects and the routines explored in another chapter of the book, focused on the perimeter of houses. I looked at boundary work happening around participants' doors, windows, backyards, and sidewalks. In an analysis of how people interact around and with their trash, for instance, I demonstrated in another way what privacy meant to the people I interviewed and how they attempted to protect it in their daily lives. The stories of trash management alone—from a failed attempt at privacy when a cat paraded a used condom across the living room floor in front of guests, to the careful shredding, water-logging, and subsequent burning of medical brochures, to the stacking of recyclables on the tops of dumpsters so homeless people wouldn't leave homeowners' personal items strewn about the alley—provided remarkable insight about where and how we draw the line between public and private—as well as the useful and useless.

Umbrellas, doors, and trash are not the only things that provide an enticing window into the conceptual, classificatory frameworks that guide our everyday behaviors. We can treat other matters as "objects" and produce similar results. In *Islands of Privacy*, I also looked at secrets as if they were objects, and used hundreds of interviewees' stories to explore the lives of secrets and the work of making, keeping, revealing, and finding out about them. One could treat almost any piece of information as an object and do a "day/week/year in the life of this object" analysis. In this digital information age, so much is reduced to packets of 0s and 1s, that object mapping could be a useful approach to understanding more than just the things we can touch with our hands.

About Today's Mechanics

This challenge was to think with, about, and through your object—not around it. You don't want the object to serve simply as a place to start directing your eyes as you then drift toward watching the users—or anything else around it. If you found that you had trouble keeping your attention on the object, start any future efforts like this by focusing entirely on the object, first. Anchor yourself in the object before letting your attention go anywhere else. Next, allow yourself to notice only the moments in which the object interfaces with other objects and its users—the places and ways in which the object and other entities touch. *Then* soften your focus and move to describing how the object is used, the role it plays, and its function in the overall system you are studying.

One reason this can be problematic stems from the very reason that focusing on an object is such an excellent entry point for a fieldworker. Any object in your field site, like any person found there, is part of a system. The object, the users, the environment—these are all parts of one big system. The object is, in fact, a clue to the whole of which it is a part.

As a fieldworker, you want to be able to focus solely or in any combination you want on any aspect of the system. You should be able to describe an individual, an individual's actions, an object, and the ways the object interfaces with any other individual or object, in equal detail—as well as (eventually, if you had enough time) the entirety of the system in which each of these is a part. When it comes to objects, this will let you discover the singular or multiple affordances of the object, the purposes it meets as well as those it does not, and its current and potential roles in the system. The ability to look down on the system of which the object is a part is also vital—to comprehend the whole as well as an isolated component. Whether detailed, close reflection on one piece of the system, or a systematic, bird's-eye view of its entirety, we need to be able to sustain our focus on whatever we want, whenever we want.

Overall, Exercise 8 was another great opportunity to focus on the "how" question. In this case, the question was how the object was constructed and how it was used during your observation session. The exercise was also designed to help you approach the field with a mindset determined to extract all the insight possible during your observation session. Downtime is meditation time, thinking deeply time in the field on whatever—or whoever—is there. Apply this approach to anything you see and you can significantly up your game as a fieldworker. Many students welcome this kind of engagement with the field, feeling drained but also refreshed by the unexpected insights that result.

You may want to level up the challenge of this exercise by observing an object under more constant use. If so, you may wish to engage in interval research to map the activity you see. For something used constantly, sampling what's going on rather than trying to capture everything could give you excellent insight without becoming overwhelmed.

About the Write-Up

Some of the most satisfying insights from this exercise have to do with how object use reveals larger patterns of space use and engagement with the environment, as well as the uniqueness of individuals as they interact with objects and demonstrate their relationships with each other. Remember that the raw data are only the beginning of your process. Extracting higher-level insights is the ultimate goal. Photos of the object, for instance, and how it was used during your observation should not be mistaken for—or used in place of—an *analysis* of the object and its uses. Rather, they should support your analysis. To see examples of this point and others, I recommend looking at some of the analyses done by others who have tackled this exercise.

Sample responses to this exercise and brief comments about them may found at http://global.oup.com/us/watchingclosely.

Exercise Nine—
Object Mapping II—Play

This last official exercise focuses again on objects in the field. This time, however, we're going to add a concept to your mission: play. Looking for instances of play is an excellent pedagogical exercise for fieldworkers because it makes us realize that any activity we might observe is fundamentally defined by its analytical framing. Be patient with yourself because this exercise shows just how difficult it can be to understand an activity simply by observing it. It is an excellent reminder of the remarkable challenge of the ethnographic enterprise—and what anthropologist Clifford Geertz (1973, 7) described as the "piled-up structures of inference and implication through which an ethnographer is continually trying to pick his way."

This exercise uses the conceptual framework for thinking about play that I offered in my article "Boundary Play" (2005). Here, I argued that cognitive boundaries are manifested in and through spatial ones, and both provide a distinct opportunity for play among those who share similar understandings of cultural categories. This form of play begins with shared cultural assumptions of what is normal, then gives them a twist, to make them a source of amusement. We see this from kids playing in and around a dog crate as well as the environmental features of theme restaurants and buildings like Chicago's Shedd Aquarium.

The article was a straightforward application of the mission-driven, concept-based, empirical approach to fieldwork this book advocates. "Play" is a more difficult example of the approach, though, as an especially challenging concept for a fieldworker. To do observation research about play, a researcher must first understand what constitutes "play" in the minds of her or his subjects. We have to be able to identify play—and "not-play"—when we see it.

The problem is that play is not defined so much by activities as by the meaning attributed to them, that is, the manner in which the activities are interpreted by those engaged in them. Typically, we would turn to interviews and participant observation to learn the meanings actors attribute to their actions. The point of this exercise, however, is to see how far you can get in discerning meaning just by watching closely.

To explore the nature—and fragility—of play, we should begin with sociologist Gregory Bateson's work in *Steps to an Ecology of Mind* (2000 [1955]). In his essay "A Theory of Play and Fantasy," Bateson offers a splendid analysis of play as a shared understanding or "framing" of activity. When we play, both human and nonhuman animals use various forms of "metacommunication" to let each other know that our actions constitute play—not the serious, "real thing" that the play references. "The playful nip denotes the bite," Bateson writes, "but it does not denote what would be denoted by the bite" (180).

Sociologist Erving Goffman then expands on Bateson's concept in *Frame Analysis* (1977), my favorite of Goffman's work. Framing, Goffman argues, is a basic sociocognitive process. Any strip of activity may be understood from multiple interpretive frameworks. The meaning of the actual, objective facts happening in front of us depends on the frame we put around it, the interpretive lens through which we view it.

We learn which frame to use in order to understand an observed strip of activity through socialization. We learn to pick up on nuanced, detailed behavior, as well as more noticeable factors like the physical setting, the time of day, and the demographics of the actors to select the appropriate framing for correctly interpreting what we see. Whenever we watch an interaction and can't tell if the individuals are playing or fighting, for instance, the problem is we can't tell which sociocognitive framing of the activity we should use to interpret what we're seeing.

Good defense attorneys understand the importance and power of how activities are framed. When faced with irrefutable evidence about their clients they do not waste time challenging it. Instead, they argue it was not an intentional crime and offer alternative framings for why their clients did it. "It was an accident." "It was self-defense." "It was a prank." Or, paraphrasing a case in the papers some years ago, "Your Honor," the defense attorney argued, "my client did indeed sell those drugs to that person. However, earlier in the week my client was approached by someone identifying himself as an FBI agent. This individual asked for my client's assistance in an investigation. My client agreed to pretend to sell drugs to what turned out to be a local undercover narcotics officer because he believed he was helping a government agent in a sting operation." It was a most innovative attempt indeed to provide an alternative framing of what happened.

In our own lives we often think we know exactly what's going on, only to find out we're dead wrong. Even when we think the facts are clear, we find out we've chosen the wrong frame with which to interpret them. Sometimes this happens by design. (Comedians as well as con men love to play with framing expectations.) Sometimes we select the wrong frame because we did not know about an alternative. (Imagine a child walking in on a consensual sexual bondage scene.) Sometimes we use the wrong lens because the alternative never occurred to us. (She isn't fighting with him because she hates him; she's deeply attracted to him!)

With all the ways and times we can get framing wrong, it amazes me how often we get the framing right.

Correctly identifying "play" is no exception. In *With the Boys* (1987), Gary Alan Fine's excellent ethnography of Little League baseball, the author addresses this exact problem. Little League has a rich history of criticism based on the activity's organized, competitive, adult-driven nature. Are these children really having fun and choosing to do this, or is Little League a soul-crushing activity that the parents force on their kids? In a nutshell, is this play or is it work?

Fine answers that it's sport, and sport has elements of both. It feels like work when things are not going well, and when the players don't want to be there. It feels like play, however, when it's fun and the kids enjoy spending their time together. Little League activities in and of themselves have no fixed meaning; they are defined by the frame an individual puts around those activities.

Play is a frame that can be highly localized and it can therefore be a tough concept to see in action. Play requires a fairly deep understanding of the sociocognitive world of your subjects. If you study a different species or a group with its own culture, trying to identify play lets you quickly realize the extent to which you are and are not a fully socialized insider.

Play can be a fragile frame, too. Hit just a little too hard, tease just a little too much, win just a little too big, and it's like someone threw a switch. For an observer to see that happening not only requires a solid understand of what play is, but it also requires an ability to discern precisely when a decision was made that allowed the play to continue or brought it to a grinding halt.

A combination of Theodore Kemper's (2011) work on status and sociologist Jack Katz's (2001) argument in *How Emotions Work* suggests an interesting explanation for the fragility of play. Kemper argues that our own status is a function of the social groups to which we belong and their relative standing compared to other social groups. He further argues that what we think of as funny (or, I would argue, playful) depends primarily on the normative allocation and negotiation of status among these social groups. An individual laughs at something, Kemper says, because it validates their status to do so. They identify with the status-victory implied by the amusing story, joke, or situation while simultaneously proving they "get it." Should an individual *not* get it (proving they are not "in the know," that is, not a privileged insider) or think the story/joke/situation demeans them—reducing their status in some way—then it's not funny and not playful.

Should an individual react strongly—in any way—to a potentially funny or playful situation, Katz would argue that the reaction indicates just how much they relate to the identity-related matters it raises. The individual might laugh instantly, loudly, and in a prolonged, even hysterical fashion. They might instantly become angry or even violent. Either way, such a strong emotional response signals a person for whom their past, present, and future identities have come crashing together.

Katz's analysis is fully consistent with Kemper's status-based theories of interactions. Recall Kemper's argument that we generally are more driven by the desire to not lose status than we are to gain it. It makes perfect sense that the moment a player thinks the play results in a loss of their status, they will instantly switch to a far more serious frame of mind.

The ability to see the frame of play—much less when it breaks—is a worthy challenge for any fieldworker. It can be hard enough to identify behavior as play or not-play in humans. It can be especially difficult for those who are studying another species. If play exists in the mind of the actor, visibly signaled through highly nuanced behaviors, it can take quite a bit of experience observing another species before one feels confident interpreting their activities.

You might find it useful to think about another aspect of play for this exercise. Whether psychologists or zoologists, animal behaviorists of all kinds agree that play has at least one distinctive function. Through play, the young practice and acquire the roles, skills, and relationships they will need to survive. Some additional clues that might help you decipher play or not play then, are (1) if at least one of the individuals engaged in a potentially playful activity is young (or "young at heart") and (2) if the activity does not seem to have any immediate, specific, survival-related purpose at this time, but it could provide such an advantage one day.

Today's Exercise

Identify instances of play in your subjects' activities. Describe these instances carefully and explain why you think the activity constitutes play. What are your clues that this is the frame of play and not something else? How is it different, in other words, from other, nonplay activities that you observe?

Watch especially for any interactions with objects (fixed-feature and others) in the course of playful activity. What objects seem to be most important for play activity? Which objects seem least important for play?

You can think very direct and at a detailed level here. You can also think at a higher level in which you force yourself to consider every single object in the field and how it enables any of the play you witness, even if it doesn't seem to be directly involved in a particular interaction.

What happens if you treat other individuals as objects, in this respect? Are there any individuals in the group who seem more or less central for the activity of play? Are any specific individuals more or less central to certain kinds of play?

I recommend that you do not read further until you have completed this exercise, including the report based on your fieldwork.

No more intrn btw Suzie & Azizi
Still w/in 1 Foot

then Azizi moves to right side
of balcony

SUZIE   AZIZI

laying on
Rightside

2 limbs on
branch

sits up
facing

4 limbs on
• Bjects

Play Time: Observing Jojo's Troop

I decided that while observing, the dichotomy of play/not
play is everywhere if one looks close enough. Really getting
down and saying some behavior may or not be play is in the
eye of the beholder. One has to see how the ape is doing
something, because one person may call it play while
another says it is not play; to truly distinguish, one would
have to know the mental mindset of the ape in that
moment in time. at what point is any strip of activity truly
a constant running without perhaps small break here and
there, and is one long engagement truly all play or does it
not also have some periods of extreme-non play, perhaps
signals to another individual telling it it had crossed a sort
of boundary?

Post-Exercise Discussion

About Today's Concept

A careful response to Exercise 9 may have a lot of doubt woven through it. Many students turn to video recording—or a wish for video recording—for this exercise, in part because they want to re-visit what they saw as they try to decide if it was play. As fieldworkers, we can be extremely—in fact, overly—confident when it comes to "knowing" what we're seeing, so it is good to challenge our own classifications of what we see. It will help us make our claims more carefully. We will likely become far more imaginative in how we interpret what we see and generate more interesting and correct insights, as well. This exercise was designed to help you question the use of conventional labels for what you see in the field and become capable of treating everything as if it is as doubtful and difficult to see as "play."

About the Mechanics of This Exercise

Did you see any instances of play? Did you see any instances in which the frame of play was broken by something going awry? If you didn't—or not as many instances as you wished—don't worry. This could be disappointing at one level, but it should not get in the way of either your observation session or the usefulness of your write-up. Remember to take the absence as well as the presence of something as a great excuse to think about it.

If you did not see much—or even any—play going on, there may be many possible reasons. Maybe there was no play happening. Maybe individuals were playing, but you missed the cues that your subjects transmitted, defining their activity as play to each other. Maybe they were playing, but you literally couldn't see the play because they were sending funny jokes or flirting via email, playing a game on their cell phone, or some such. Or maybe play was going on, but neither you nor your subjects knew it. Your subjects' bosses/children/wait staff could have been playing a game with them—and with you—unbeknownst to any of you! This last might seem a bit of a reach, but you should always try to think creatively when diagnosing any unexpected results in your fieldwork.

No matter how much play you think you observed, ideally, you should have paid as much attention to the objects you observed this time as you did last time, layering the attention to play over that. In the process, it is important to find a way to separate your detailed descriptions of the interactions you saw (including, perhaps, how a given object was manipulated) from your reflections on whether or not you believed the activity to be play or not-play. Good note-taking is essential, as you must not only capture the nuances of what you see but also of what you think about it. This will let you make an effective case later for the frame that you believe was in use. This is precisely how this approach to fieldwork promotes the theory-testing and theory-generation that can put fieldworkers in an excellent position to take their discipline to new places.

On Today's Write-Up

This exercise provides an especially good opportunity to think of interesting ways to slice and re-slice, then re-present your data. The raw data are usually quite interesting, in and of itself. So are the ways you might choose to reorganize what you saw. Perhaps you decided to order your findings according to the objects that appear most and least important for play (including those on which individuals stand, sit, or otherwise locate themselves during the play); by individual, looking at who is the most playful and what each individual plays with and for how long; or by the solo versus collective nature of play, who seems to prefer which, and what objects are associated with either, and how.

This exercise also gives you an excellent chance to play with different ways of re-presenting your data, in light of your analysis. Charts, diagrams, and pictorial depictions of accumulated interactions can be particularly useful. Great data, great analysis, and great re-presentations of your data to support your analysis add up to great fieldwork.

This exercise is also a chance to get even better at thinking about the multiple uses and meanings of a given object, as well as how thinking with an object can illuminate a bigger picture. Fieldworkers should constantly read in design, architecture, anthropology and archeology, religion, psychology, art and art history, technology studies, and the like for new ways of thinking about objects, the social and material attributes and expectations manifested in them, and the roles they play in the lives of individuals, groups, historical periods, and places. So many disciplines have done so much work on objects that we need not reinvent the wheel to find a unique way to use it in our work. Use it we should, though, for not only is anything we find in the field fair game to think with; if it's there, then we are obligated to do so.

Sample responses to this final exercise may be found at http://global.oup.com/us/watchingclosely.

Part Three:
Moving Forward

How to Use This Book Going Forward

After I began working with design students I was struck by the advantages that their drawing, painting, and visual modeling held for fieldworkers. It seemed to me that my students weren't just depicting their subjects, but they were coming to understand them this way, too. I wanted to experience that. I decided to take an introductory drawing class at my local arts center.

Almost immediately I encountered two major problems in my drawing class. Both relate to the same problem that my own observation course addresses: how to better see and then re-present what we see. I never imagined that my attempt to learn what I thought was a fairly distinctive skill would reveal so much about the ethnographic enterprise.

The first problem was that I produced drawings of people and objects that looked like cartoons—perfectly proportioned, two-dimensional caricatures of the real thing. Halfway through the second class my instructor, Ben Rubin, came to the rescue. I had the process all wrong. "You are not drawing a person," I remember him saying. "You are not drawing an object. You are capturing the light scattering off them."

Bingo! Three-dimensionality was my new best friend. With that advice, drawing felt like something I was born to do. I now looked not at the object, but at the patterns of light that defined it. My new drawings were indeed "light years" away from what I had been doing.

Feeling like the problem was solved, I turned to our homework assignment for the next week: spend one hour drawing an object. It could be anything. On a lovely summer day I headed to the backyard. The kids' wagon was standing up against the fence, its wheels sticking out. I chose a wheel and went to work but could not produce a realistic rendering to save my life. I couldn't get the symmetry right. I spent almost two hours trying to do the assignment and finally gave up when I ran out of time. I showed up at class the next day frustrated and embarrassed.

I wasn't the only newbie with that particular problem, however, and so our clever instructor gave us all a tip: Next time, drape a piece of fabric over the object. Cover half of it, then try again. Walla! Sure enough, I came to class the next week with a most satisfactory, three-dimensional charcoal drawing of half of a Flexible Flyer wheel.

One way of describing the problem in both situations was that part of my brain "knew" this thing I was trying to draw and it kept overriding my ability to actually see it. This part of my brain wanted me to draw what I *thought* I saw, what I *thought* this thing looked like. Because I was so certain of what I was seeing and how I was surely supposed to capture it on paper, I couldn't actually see it and I couldn't actually capture it at all.

To really see my subjects I had to learn how to alienate myself from them. I had to find a way to stop thinking I knew what I was looking at and how I should be doing so. I had to see the thing as a pattern of scattered light or as a disembodied, fragment of an unknown thing. Only then could I see my subject and then re-present it in a much more accurate and useful fashion.

In short, I had to learn how to make something familiar into something unfamiliar, how to focus on only one aspect of it and forget about the rest, to treat each moment of a thing as the only one that mattered, for now, while also keeping its broader context in mind. Once that happened, I could really look at something,

I could actually draw it, and, when I was done—having touched every part of it in this new way, with my eyes—I could finally see it, appreciate it, in a whole new light.

Needless to say, I was stunned when I realized that my teacher had just helped me do the same thing that I was trying to help others do, in the very course that led me to take his. We both wanted to help our students see things in a new way, and to do so as a result of trying to capture and re-present them in new ways too.

I still have my drawing pads from that class. Every once in a while, I rediscover them. I enjoy flipping through the pages, looking at the transformation of my work during that adventure.

Well? How did you do with this adventure? If you line up every one of your reports, every exercise worth of notes, how has your work changed? How has your view of the field and of the ethnographic enterprise changed?

Hopefully, you now have a remarkable collection of artifacts, each a small but important step in your journey as a fieldworker. If you have been diligent, reflective, and honest, you should be rightfully proud of your responses, providing a wonderful window into your research process. And whoever or whatever you studied while working through this book, you are likely to not only have excellent insight about yourself, as a researcher, but also about the species that you examined so closely.

So what's next? How might you use this book going forward? Of course you should reread it and redo the exercises as often as you like. You may find it a great way to keep developing your skill set. You should also exchange and discuss your results with others. There's no better way to identify and build on what works well and become more aware of other innovative approaches. As the writer and artist Austin Kleon (2012, 2014) reminds us, if we mean to get better at it, there are good reasons to share our best ideas and show our work to each other.

Most important, I hope you will use what you found here as inspiration for your own fieldwork and any future projects you take on. Developing a mission for the day that combines a concept-based agenda with another focus—like a focus on time, space, or an object—can be an especially fruitful way to take the work you've done for this book and move forward. You can apply this approach to any concept you want, any behavior in which you are interested. Gender, race, family, work, love, religion, deviance, trust, risk, norms, advocacy, efficiency—find ways to turn the concepts that are central to your work into observational missions that you can achieve during your days in the field. You might even take some of your favorite works, some of the classics in your discipline, and try to turn each of them into an exercise (or series of them), just for the fun of it.

You can develop missions for yourself based on hypotheses that you wish to test, too. The level of confidence one might have in the validity of one's data and conclusions will differ from a hypothesis explored through a statistically representative data set. However, within commonsense limitations, it is possible to pursue certain kinds of specific, testable questions using observation-based research, and to design missions and days in the field around these points of entry.

That's exactly what sociologists Harvey Molotch, Noah McClain, and I did during three of my all-time favorite days in the field. Our overarching goal was to think about security in the New York subway system.[1] Each day, we decided on a specific question we wanted to answer, each of which would lead us toward this goal.

On our first day working together, McClain explained that most New York subway trains are as long as a football field and take two people to operate. One person is up front driving the train (the operator) while the other (the conductor) is in the middle. The conductor manages the loading and unloading of passengers, sticking her head out the train window to make sure that no one has a limb caught in the closing doors or—a deadly scenario—between the train and the platform before the train starts moving. Molotch then described the Metropolitan Transportation Authority (MTA) initiative to design a subway car that could run without a conductor and that also would not hurt a passenger who was either caught in the doors or determined to hold them open. The MTA had decided this hugely expensive enterprise was a top priority because, they claimed, passengers held the doors open for each other and delayed the trains.

So, for one day—amid all the other information washing over us as we rode the subway—we chose to forefront a twofold question: (1) Are trains delayed leaving the platforms, and (2) if so, was it because passengers held the doors open for each other?

We did see trains regularly delayed in their departures, though by a matter of seconds. But it was *conductors* holding the doors open and delaying departures, albeit in very efficient ways. Looking out their centrally located windows, they held the train for mobility-impaired passengers, for those just arriving on another train and needing to transfer (so no one would run and get hurt in this dangerous place), and to answer questions and give directions to confused riders on the platform. We saw one occasion that day in which passengers held the door for each other—a bunch of giggling, shrieking teenage girls in school uniforms held the door for their friend bringing up the rear. But mostly, with compassion and expert knowledge (and sometimes an eye for an especially attractive passenger), the conductors delayed the trains and they did so to compensate for a very user-unfriendly system. In fact, our day produced a lengthy list of the ways the system failed its riders and resulted in the conductors having to use their discretion for it to function.

On another day, McClain and I looked for a mission for just the two of us. I asked him if there was a nagging, unanswered question he had about something he'd seen. There was. He had noticed that each driver would make some kind of a gesture just before they opened the train doors. He hadn't had a chance to figure out why yet, so we made that our mission for the day. Could we find out, through observation alone, why the drivers made these gestures when they pulled up to the platform?

We had a great deal of deductive fun trying to solve this mystery while taking in everything else around us. Although we didn't know why they were doing it, we repeatedly observed how stylish and individual the drivers' gestures were each time they pulled into the station. One bent his elbow, raised his hand 90 degrees, and then brought it down, straightening his arm to point out the window in a definite, precise way. Another flung a casual, backhanded wave out his window. A third flicked a single, stunningly manicured and long-nailed finger toward the window as she stopped her train.

We never did figure it out, not that day. It was only later, when McClain interviewed drivers, that he found the answer. During our travels, McClain had pointed out a yellow and black zebra-striped line of tape, wood, or paint in the middle of each platform. It turns out that drivers are required to pull up to this marker each time they stop the train. They must then physically acknowledge and confirm to the conductors—via the distinctive gestures we'd seen—that the train was stopped in the right position along the platform and, once the doors opened, no passenger would step out into a void.

This is a wonderful example of why observation, alone, is rarely enough for fieldworkers to answer their questions. However, this collection of images—highly unlikely to be obtained in any other way—became an interesting set of data points for the overall project. An important theme of McClain's work is how individual employees comply with MTA procedures. The variation in gestures illustrated how such compliance could be personalized. The gestures also became part of the interviews McClain conducted. They served as an excellent entry point for lengthy conversations about how compliance-based work performance is measured and managed for these employees.

On the last of our three days riding the rails together, we asked ourselves a final, higher-level question: Based solely on what we observed, when it came to security in the subway, what, exactly, was being secured and protected down there?

We stood on platforms, watching and thinking with the machinery, the built environment, and the people coming and going around us. We got on and off many trains; listened to garbled PA systems; counted detailed notices about schedule and track changes in tiny print with lengthy explanations in English, only; watched people with strollers, little children, packages, high heels, and arthritis negotiate the gates and stairs. We watched dismayed mothers, separated from their children, as they tried to figure out why their new 10-fare cards would not let them through. We saw MTA and NYPD officers on patrol, workers trying to see out of booths covered with notices, panhandlers and schizophrenics pestering riders, and cleaning staff trying to keep up with assorted noxious substances.

By the end of the day, we concluded that what was being protected, first and foremost, was the fare. The physical infrastructure—trains, platforms, and equipment of all kinds—was next. It was a toss-up as to whether the workers in the subway system or the passengers came after that. We agreed, however, that, prima facie, concern for the security of people definitely seemed to have a lower priority than that of the fare, the objects, and the built environment.

All in all, our three-day sojourn confirmed that a single, well-informed, well-formulated question can provide a very doable mission for the day. It can advance one's fieldwork most effectively. And it can do all this in an energizing, highly rewarding way.

Our work in the subway also showed how easy it is to take the approach proposed in this book and put it to work in pursuit of successful, user-centered design. For my students, for instance, the value of the work they've been kind enough to share with this book's readers doesn't end with their responses to these exercises. I also ask them to use the data and insights they've gathered during the exercises to propose new, user-centered design concepts to benefit the troop of gorillas they've been watching most closely.

Students identify a problem or opportunity based on their observations (e.g., a toy, tool, schedule, or environmental feature), gather additional data, analyze the likely intended and unintended outcomes from implementing their design for each of the affected stakeholders, and propose a research plan for assessing the success or failure of this hypothetical design. Thus, these students have an opportunity to learn the basics of how to design from the field—and from observational data, specifically—and to use the possibilities of this kind of research to minimize the risks associated with the unknown implications of new designs as well as future improved iterations of those designs.

Conclusion

Ethnographers can't get all the answers to all our questions using only observation. Ethnography is a three-legged stool for a good reason. Conversation, participation, and observation are each necessary for us to do our work. However, I hope that this book has shown that observation, alone, can be a powerful addition to one's ethnographic toolkit. If we take advantage of this tool more often, I believe our work can only get better—especially if we share our efforts with each other. If each of us questions, innovates, and incorporates others' excellent efforts into our own, we surely can take fieldwork farther and faster into the 21st century.

This is, in fact, my overarching goal for *Watching Closely*: to encourage all fieldworkers, from the broadest possible spectrum of disciplines and professions, to develop ever-more diverse and dynamic toolkits as well as new ways of using them. We each need to make an active, personal commitment to ethnography's future. We should not settle simply for perfecting the methods of the past but instead strive to be the innovators who will take our methods forward.

Note

1. Molotch's provocative work on this and the many other aspects of security that he studied for this project appear in *Against Security* (2012). McClain's insights are also found here as well as in his 2011 dissertation thesis, "The Institutions of Urban Anxiety: Work, Organizational Process and Security Practice in the New York Subway."

Augustin, Sally, and Cindy Coleman. *The Designer's Guide to Doing Research: Applying Knowledge in Practice for Design Excellence*. Hoboken, NJ: John Wiley & Sons, 2012.

Bateson, Gregory. "A Theory of Play and Fantasy." In *Steps to an Ecology of Mind: Collected Essays in Anthropology, Psychiatry, Evolution, and Epistemology*. Chicago: University of Chicago Press, 2000, 177–193.

Becker, Howard Saul. "Concepts." In *Tricks of the Trade: How to Think about Your Research While You're Doing It*. Chicago: University of Chicago Press, 1998, 109–145.

Becker, Howard Saul. Unpublished paper. "How to Find Out How to Do Qualitative Research." April 2009. http://home.earthlink.net/~hsbecker/articles/NSF.html.

Bell, Genevieve, Mark Blythe, and Phoebe Sengers. "Making by Making Strange: Defamiliarization and the Design of Domestic Technology." *ACM Transactions on Computer-Human Interaction* 12, no. 2 (2005): 149–173.

Berger, Peter L., and Thomas Luckmann. *The Social Construction of Reality; a Treatise in the Sociology of Knowledge*. Garden City, NY: Doubleday, 1968.

Bhaskar, Roy. *A Realist Theory of Science*. Leeds: Leeds Books, 1975.

Blumer, Herbert. "What Is Wrong with Social Theory?" *American Sociological Review* 19, no. 1 (1954): 3–10.

Brajuha, Mario, and Lyle Hallowell. "Legal Intrusion and the Politics of Fieldwork." *Journal of Contemporary Ethnography* 14, no. 4 (1986): 454–478.

Chase, Ivan. "Vacancy Chains." *Annual Review of Sociology* 17, no. 5 (1991): 133–154.

Collins, Randall. *Interaction Ritual Chains*. Princeton, NJ: Princeton University Press, 2004.

Corte, de Real, Eduardo. *The Smooth Guide to Travel Drawing*. Lisbon: Livros Horizonte, 2009.

Csikszentmihalyi, Mihaly. *Beyond Boredom and Anxiety: Experiencing Flow at Work and Play*. San Francisco: Jossey-Bass, 1975.

Csikszentmihalyi, Mihaly, and Rick Emery Robinson. *The Art of Seeing: An Interpretation of the Aesthetic Encounter*. Los Angeles: J. Paul Getty Museum, 1990.

Emerson, Robert M., Rachel I. Fretz, and Linda Shaw. *Writing Ethnographic Fieldnotes*. Chicago: University of Chicago Press, 1995.

Fine, Gary Alan. "Little League as Sport and Play." In *With the Boys: Little League Baseball and Preadolescent Culture*. Chicago: University of Chicago Press, 1987, 43–60.

Fleck, Ludwik. *Genesis and Development of a Scientific Fact*. Chicago: University of Chicago Press, 1981.

Geertz, Clifford. "Thick Description: Toward an Interpretive Theory of Culture." In *The Interpretation of Cultures: Selected Essays*. New York: Basic Books, 1973, 3–30.

Goffman, Erving. "Keys and Keying." In *Frame Analysis: An Essay on the Organization of Experience*. New York: Harper & Row, 1977, 40–82.

Gorski, P. S. "What Is Critical Realism? And Why Should You Care?" *Contemporary Sociology: A Journal of Reviews* 42 (2013): 658–670.

Grazian, David. "Where the Wild Things Aren't." *Sociological Quarterly* 53, no. 4 (2012): 546–565.

Grimshaw, Anna. *The Ethnographer's Eye: Ways of Seeing in Anthropology*. Cambridge: Cambridge University Press, 2001.

Hall, Edward T. *The Hidden Dimension*. Garden City, NY: Doubleday, 1966.

Halloran, Andrew. *Song of the Ape: Understanding the Languages of Chimpanzees*. New York: St. Martin's Press, 2012.

Horowitz, Alexandra. *On Looking: A Walker's Guide to the Art of Observation*. New York: Scribner, 2014.

Katz, Jack. "Analytic Induction." In *International Encyclopedia of the Social and Behavioral Sciences*, edited by Neil J. Smelser and Paul Baltes. Oxford: Elsevier, 2001, 480–484.

Katz, Jack. *How Emotions Work*. Chicago: University of Chicago Press, 1999.

Kemper, Theodore D. *Status, Power and Ritual Interaction a Relational Reading of Durkheim, Goffman and Collins*. Burlington, VT: Ashgate, 2011.

Kleon, Austin. *Show Your Work!: 10 Ways to Share Your Creativity and Get Discovered*. New York: Workman, 2014.

Kleon, Austin. *Steal Like an Artist: 10 Things Nobody Told You about Being Creative*. New York: Workman, 2012.

Kontopoulos, Kyriakos. Unpublished Dissertation. *The Making of an Authoritarian Regime: Greece, 1944–1974*. Cambridge: Harvard University, 1976.

Kuhn, Thomas S. *The Structure of Scientific Revolutions*. 2nd ed. Chicago: University of Chicago Press, 1970 [1962].

Lamont, Michele, and Ann Swidler. "Methodological Pluralism and the Possibilities and Limits of Interviewing." *Qualitative Sociology* 37 (2014): 153–171.

Latour, Bruno. *Reassembling the Social: An Introduction to Actor-Network-Theory*. Oxford: Oxford University Press, 2005.

Lofland, J. "Analytic Ethnography: Features, Failings, and Futures." *Journal of Contemporary Ethnography* (1995): 30–67.

Lofland, Lyn H. "Control by Design." In *The Public Realm: Exploring the City's Quintessential Social Territory*. Hawthorne, NY: Aldine De Gruyter, 1998.

Lukes, Steven. *Power: A Radical View*. London: Macmillan, 1974.

Lury, Celia, and Nina Wakeford. *Inventive Methods: The Happening of the Social*. London: Routledge, 2014.

Mannheim, Karl. *Structures of Thinking*. Edited by David Kettler, Volker Meja, and Nico Stehr. London: Routledge & Kegan Paul, 1982.

Martin, John Levi. *The Explanation of Social Action*. Oxford: Oxford University Press, 2011.

McClain, Noah. Unpublished dissertation. "The Institutions of Urban Anxiety: Work, Organizational Process and Security Practice in the New York Subway." New York: New York University, 2011.

McCloud, Scott. *Understanding Comics: The Invisible Art*. New York: HarperPerennial, 1994.

Milgram, Stanley. "Psychological Maps of Paris." In *The Individual in a Social World*, ed. Thomas Blass. London: Pinter and Martin, 2010 [1977], 77–99.

Mills, C. Wright. *The Sociological Imagination*. New York: Oxford University Press, 1959.

Molotch, Harvey Luskin. *Where Stuff Comes From: How Toasters, Toilets, Cars, Computers, and Many Other Things Come to Be as They Are*. New York: Routledge, 2003.

Molotch, Harvey Luskin, and Laura Noren, eds. *Toilet: Public Restrooms and the Politics of Sharing*. New York: New York University Press, 2010.

Molotch, Harvey Luskin. *Against Security: How We Go Wrong at Airports, Subways, and Other Sites of Ambiguous Danger*. Princeton, NJ: Princeton University Press, 2012.

Napier, Mick. *Improvise: Scene from the Inside Out*. Portsmouth, NH: Heinemann, 2004.

Nippert-Eng, Christena. "Boundary Play." *Space and Culture* 8, no. 3 (2005): 302–324.

Nippert-Eng, Christena, et al. *Gorillas Up Close*. New York: Henry Holt, 2016.

Nippert-Eng, Christena E. *Home and Work Negotiating Boundaries through Everyday Life*. Chicago: University of Chicago Press, 1996.

Nippert-Eng, Christena E. *Islands of Privacy*. Chicago: University of Chicago Press, 2010.

Nippert-Eng, Christena E. "'Mommy, Mommy,' or 'Excuse Me, Ma'am': Gender and Interruptions at Home and Work" (unpublished winner, 1993 ASA Culture Section Graduate Student Paper Competition).

Ocejo, Richard E., ed. *Ethnography and the City: Readings on Doing Urban Fieldwork*. New York: Routledge, 2013.

Park, Robert E. "Human Migration and the Marginal Man." *American Journal of Sociology* 33, no. 6 (1928): 881.

Perlow, Leslie A. *Finding Time: How Corporations, Individuals, and Families Can Benefit from New Work Practices*. Ithaca, NY: ILR Press, 1997.

Popper, Karl R. *The Logic of Scientific Discovery*. New York: Routledge, 2002 [1935].

Purnell, Carolyn. *Enlightened Bodies*. New York: W.W. Norton Company: forthcoming.

Ragin, Charles C., and Howard Saul Becker. *What Is a Case? Exploring the Foundations of Social Inquiry*. New York: Cambridge University Press, 1992.

Roth, Julius A. *Timetables: Structuring the Passage of Time in Hospital Treatment and Other Careers*. Indianapolis, IN: Bobbs-Merrill, 1963.

Salvador, Tony, Genevieve Bell, and Ken Anderson. "Design Ethnography." *Design Management Journal* 10, no. 3 (2010): 35–41.

Schwartz, Barry. "The Stratification of Waiting." In *Queuing and Waiting: Studies in the Social Organization of Access and Delay*. Chicago: University of Chicago Press, 1975.

Sommer, Robert. *Personal Space: The Behavioral Basis of Design*. Upper Saddle River, NJ: Prentice-Hall, 1969.

Tuan, Yi-Fu. *Space and Place: The Perspective of Experience*. Minneapolis: University of Minnesota Press, 2001 [1977].

Tufte, Edward. *Envisioning Information*. Cheshire, CT: Graphics Press, 1990.

Van Maanen, John. *Tales of the Field: On Writing Ethnography*. Chicago: University of Chicago Press, 2010 [1988].

Vaughan, Diane. "Ethnographic Analytics." In *The Oxford Handbook of Analytical Sociology*. New York: Oxford University Press, 2009, 688–711.

Wade, Nicholas. "Anthropology a Science? Statement Deepens a Rift." *New York Times*, December 9, 2010. http://www.nytimes.com/2010/12/10/science/10anthropology.html.

Zerubavel, Eviatar. "If Simmel Were a Fieldworker: On Formal Sociological Theory and Analytical Field Research." *Symbolic Interaction* 3, no. 2 (1980): 25–34.

Zerubavel, Eviatar. *Hidden Rhythms: Schedules and Calendars in Social Life*. Chicago: University of Chicago Press, 1981.

Zerubavel, Eviatar. *The Seven Day Circle: The History and Meaning of the Week*. New York: Free Press, 1985.

Zerubavel, Eviatar. *Social Mindscapes: An Invitation to Cognitive Sociology*. Cambridge, MA: Harvard University Press, 1999.

Zerubavel, Eviatar. *The Elephant in the Room: Silence and Denial in Everyday Life*. Oxford: Oxford University Press, 2006.

INDEX

Figures and notes are indicated by f and n following the page number. Reproduced field notes are indicated by italic page numbers.